SCOTLAND'S AIRLINES

SCOTLAND'S AIRLINES

Charles Woodley

First published 2008

The History Press
Cirencester Road, Chalford,
Stroud, Gloucestershire, GL6 8PE
www.thehistorypress.co.uk

British Library Cataloguing in Publication Data.
A catalogue record for this book is available from the British Library.

ISBN 978 0 7524 4522 9

Typesetting and origination by The History Press
Printed in Great Britain

CONTENTS

ACKNOWLEDGEMENTS

Many people have kindly helped me with this book, and I would like to thank:

Captain J.C. Olive, for BEA images and anecdotes.

Captain Alan Whitfield, for Loganair recollections and photos.

Kieran Murray, for supplying so many Shetland photos.

Graham Osborn at Air-Britain, for sourcing and supplying photographs from the Air-Britain monochrome photo library.

Iain Hutchison, for allowing me to reproduce Loganair route maps from his excellent book *The Story of Loganair*.

Phil Lo Bao, for allowing me to use material from his book *An Illustrated History of British European Airways*.

Ian Bruce at *The Shetland News*, for permission to reproduce images of the Loganair farewell tour of the Outer Isles of Shetland.

The late John Begg, for supplying reminiscences of his time with Peregrine Air Services and Aberdeen Airways, photographs and brochures.

The public relations staff at Eastern Airways, for permission to use their images.

Robin Mackenzie, for anecdotes and photos of his time with British Airways at Stornoway.

Willy Mason, for the material on Scottish Airlines.

Elly Jones at CityStar Airlines, for supplying press cuttings and the trip to Norway.

Iain C. Mackay and Rod Simpson, for many BEA images.

J.L. Davies, archivist at the British Airways Heritage Collection, for his time and the press cuttings.

Les Sarjeant, for the many images supplied.

Brian Harwood.

Mrs June Scott.

ACKNOWLEDGEMENTS

Doreen Currie.

Robert Hooper.

Colin Frost.

Klaus Vomhof.

Lyn Lovie.

Ronald Milne.

John Ross.

David Catto.

Mrs C. Glennie.

Bob Willis.

Charles Watson.

David Castle.

Ian McFarlane.

Paul Howard, Gerry Hill, John Woodside, David Partington, Danny Grew, Wallace Shackleton and Gary Watt, all of whom allowed me to reproduce their images from the airliners.net website.

All of the Air-Britain members who responded to my appeals for information on the Air-Britain Information Exchange website (www.airbritain.com/ab-ix.html).

My wife Hazel, for her support and patience once more.

And anyone whose help I may have inadvertently not acknowledged.

I hope you find the end result worthy of all our efforts.

INTRODUCTION

The story of the airlines that provided air links within Scotland, and from Scotland to the outside world, has always been one of a struggle to maintain services to a relatively sparse population spread over a large area encompassing large cities, remote Highland points and many small islands. A great debt is owed to the pre-war pioneers of airline services, whose efforts provided the foundation for BEA and Loganair to build upon in the post-war era. In the years since, many companies have tried and failed to operate scheduled services out of Scottish airports, and the memory of the likes of Scottish Airlines, Highland Express, Aberdeen Airways and Scottish European Airways is kept alive in these pages.

At first, the inclusion of some companies may appear odd. Eastern Airways, for example, is nominally based at Humberside Airport, but it is now the second-busiest airline at Aberdeen Airport and thus a major carrier in Scotland.

BEA was Heathrow-based, but its Highlands and Islands services were operated almost as a separate entity from Glasgow.

Dan-Air's scheduled services were Gatwick-based, but its oil-related charter services from Aberdeen and Sumburgh made it a major operator there and transformed those airports. The major oil-related charter operators feature in a section devoted to this period in Scottish aviation history. The Scottish air ambulance operation was a service unique in the UK, being provided until recently by the scheduled service operators BEA and Loganair, and its story is included within these pages.

I hope this volume will serve as a fitting tribute to all those companies and individuals who worked to provide today's network of air links for the people of Scotland.

CHAPTER ONE

PRE-1947 SERVICES

HIGHLAND AIRWAYS/SCOTTISH AIRWAYS

In April 1931 Ernest Edmund Fresson and his passenger, Miss Helen Parker, flew to Orkney in DH60G Gipsy Moth G-AAWO, landing in a field near the Balfour Hospital. They were looking for a suitable landing ground from which to carry out pleasure flights that summer. These eventually commenced from Hatston Farm in early September. The following April Mr Fresson returned to Orkney, this time on an inspection visit in connection with a proposed scheduled service from Inverness to Kirkwall via Thurso and Wick, to be operated by his North British Aviation Co., which was based at Hooton Park aerodrome in Cheshire. The first leg of the journey, from Hooton Park to Edinburgh, with one passenger on board, took just under 2½ hours. At Edinburgh the passenger disembarked and was replaced by Major John D.M. Shearer, a Kirkwall resident, for the flight to Kirkwall, which took a further 2½ hours. Agreement was reached for the construction and use of a landing ground at Hatston from 1 June 1932 for the new service, and after a stay in Orkney of some 40 hours Mr Fresson flew back south, routeing via Wick, Inverness, Edinburgh and Dunbar to Liverpool.

This visit resulted in the formation of Highland Airways Ltd, which was registered in Edinburgh on 3 April 1933 'to operate air services in North East Scotland'. The initial capital was £2,625 and the chief pilot was E.E. Fresson. Among the principal shareholders was the North of Scotland Steam Navigation Co Ltd, and the chairman was the head of Macrae and Dick, well-known Inverness bus operators. Longman airfield at Inverness was selected as the operating base and named Inverness Municipal Airport, and on 8 May 1933 Highland Airways began scheduled services from Inverness to Kirkwall via Wick. The first service was operated by GA Monospar ST4 G-ACEW 'Inverness', and a single round trip was scheduled for each weekday; the total journey time each way being 1½ hours, including a 15-minute stop at Wick. The northbound services terminated at a landing ground a couple of miles from Kirkwall at Wideford Farm, which had been leased for five years for the purpose. The one-way fare was £3 3s 0, and services into Inverness were timed to connect with southbound trains from there. Three days later Highland Airways inaugurated another route, between Thurso and Kirkwall.

On 3 July 1933 the new airline suffered a setback when the Monospar crashed on approach to Kirkwall. The aircraft was badly damaged but no-one was seriously injured, and the service was able to continue while it was under repair, thanks to the generosity of John Sword of Midland and Scottish Air Ferries, another pioneer who loaned DH83 Fox Moth G-ACCT and Airspeed AS4 Ferry G-ACBT to Highland Airways. Two weeks later, Highland Airways was able to replace these with leased Monospar G-ABVN. The DH84 Dragon demonstrator G-ACCE was also evaluated on the route, leading to the purchase of DH84 G-ACIT and its entry into service on 2 August 1933.

On 7 May 1934 Highland Airways opened another new route, this time from the links at Seaton in Aberdeen to Kirkwall, using DH84 G-ACIT which had been named 'Aberdeen'

A Scottish Motor Traction pleasure flight ticket issued to Miss S. Fleming, aged four, on the occasion of her first flight, from Dyce Aerodrome, Aberdeen, on 14 April 1933. *(Mrs F. Fleming)*

E.E. Fresson in front of Monostar G-ACEW on delivery to Turnhouse on 13 April 1933.
(L.F. Sarjeant)

for the purpose. One round trip was operated each weekday. During the same month the airline was awarded the first regular airmail contract in the UK, for the carriage of mails on the Inverness-Kirkwall route. Further route expansion came on 6 August 1934, when 'on demand' services to the Orkney began. Landing strips were laid out for this purpose on Stronsay, Sanday, Hoy (Longhope), Rousay, Westray and North Ronaldsay.

For the 1935 season it was necessary for Highland Airways to find a new landing ground in Aberdeen, as the strip at Seaton was to be the site of the Highland Show during the summer. A new airfield was established at Kintore, and the Kirkwall service re-commenced from there on 24 May. Prior to this, Eric Gandar Dower, of rival Aberdeen Airways, had proposed a merger on 23 April, but this was rejected. However, in June 1935 Whitehall Securities acquired an interest and merged Highland Airways with its own Blackpool-based United Airways. The merger allowed Highland Airways to retain its identity and provided it with greater financial security, and it also brought Mr Fresson into a working agreement with George Nicholson's Northern and Scottish Airways.

Another aircraft mishap occurred on 6 September 1935 when a violent downdraft forced DH84 G-ACIT, now named 'Orcadian', into trees at Westerness on Rousay. There were no injuries to the pilot and his five passengers but the aircraft had to be dismantled and taken by boat to Kirkwall for repairs. A new twice-weekly service to Glenbrittle on Skye was inaugurated on 5 December and extended to Askernish on South Uist on 21 January 1936.

It was further extended to Sollas on North Uist on 18 March 1936, and Barra and Benbecula were also served on a charter basis.

On 3 June 1936 another new service commenced from Aberdeen (Kintore) to Lerwick via Kirkwall, with the inaugural flight operated by DH89 Dragon Rapide G-ACPN on lease from the original British Airways. Services were initially operated on Mondays, Wednesdays and Fridays, but by July the frequency had increased to six flights each week, though scaled down again for the winter months.

On 31 June 1936 Highland Airways became a wholly-owned subsidiary of Whitehall Securities and took over the Irish Sea operations of the original British Airways. Nine aircraft were transferred for this purpose, to operate on routes including Glasgow-Belfast and Liverpool-Belfast-Glasgow. On the same day, the Highland Airways Western Isles services began operating the circuit in the opposite direction on alternating weekdays. By August 1936, George Nicholson's Northern and Scottish Airways had also become part of the Whitehall Securities group of companies and was merged with Highland Airways to become Scottish Airways. E.E. Fresson kept control of operations at Inverness and George Nicholson remained in charge at Renfrew.

In May 1938 Scottish Airways commenced a Glasgow (Renfrew)-Perth-Inverness-Wick-Kirkwall-Lerwick service using DH89 Rapides, the inaugural flight being operated by G-AFEY. The fleet at that time comprised five DH84 Dragons, five Spartan Cruisers, two DH89 Rapides and a single DH Moth. At the beginning of 1939, a special meeting of the newly-formed Air Transport Licensing Authority met to resolve what it saw as wasteful competition between Scottish Airways and its principal competitor, Allied Airways, on many routes. The main loser at this hearing was Scottish Airways, which found itself virtually removed from Aberdeen routes altogether. However, an unexpected surge in business on the routes between Aberdeen, Orkney and Shetland at the beginning of 1939 saw Scottish Airways and Allied Airways co-operating to provide services between Orkney and Shetland every day except Sundays, and two daily 'ferry' services between Thurso and Kirkwall during the summer.

ABERDEEN AIRWAYS/ALLIED AIRWAYS (GANDAR DOWER)

Aberdeen Airways was registered on 2 January 1934 by Eric Leslie Gandar Dower, with an initial share capital of £8,000.

On 6 July of that year the airline took delivery of its first aircraft, DH84 Dragon G-ACRH 'Aberdonian' at its base at Dyce, Aberdeen. A week later Eric Starling was signed up as the airline's chief pilot (and only pilot at that time!) The share capital was increased to £20,000 on 20 July, and on 28 July the aerodrome at Dyce was officially opened with a flying display and air races to augment the ceremony. The airline's first scheduled service (actually a 'guest inaugural') took place on 10 September 1934 when Shorts Scion 1 G-ACUV, piloted by

Eric Starling, flew from Dyce to Renfrew with five guests. Fare-paying services started the following day, with twice-daily round trips on weekdays, but poor loads caused the service to be dropped on 24 October.

Mr Gandar Dower proposed a merger of his airline with Highland Airways on 23 April 1935, but this was rejected and so Aberdeen Airways continued along its own path, inaugurating a direct service from Dyce to Stromness (Howe) on 28 May 1935. Once again Eric Starling was in command, piloting DH84 Dragon G-ACAN on the service, which operated daily except Sundays. Henry Vallance had also joined the roster of pilots. Further expansion occurred on 4 June 1935 with the inauguration of a service between Dyce and Turnhouse aerodrome at Edinburgh. This was timed to connect at Turnhouse with the Edinburgh-Newcastle-Hull-London schedules of North Eastern Airways. Once again Eric Starling and G-ACAN did the honours on the first service, which carried no passengers. Regular services on the route were terminated on 3 August 1935 because of poor passenger loads and the lack of facilities at Turnhouse, which was still an RAF airfield, but 'on demand' flights were still operated until the summer of 1936. From 11 June 1935, a stop at Thurso (Clarendon Aerodrome) was incorporated into the Dyce-Stromness service. At the end of its first full year of operations Aberdeen Airways had carried 480 passengers and taken £1,200 in revenues, but had incurred a loss of £8,000. The Aberdeen-Thurso service was suspended for the winter on 3 December 1935, but an aircraft was stationed at Thurso to operate flights to Stromness with an 'on demand' stop at Berridale, near St Margaret's Hope on South Ronaldsay. Later, Longhope on Hoy was added as an 'on demand' stop, and at the start of 1936 another Orkney landing strip opened at Quanterness, just to the west of Kirkwall.

On 13 April 1936 the Dyce-Thurso service re-opened for the summer months, and on 2 June Aberdeen Airways inaugurated the first Aberdeen-Shetland (Sumburgh) services from Dyce, one day before E.E. Fresson commenced his Highland Airways service from Kintore. The inaugural service was flown non-stop by Eric Starling in DH89 Rapide G-ADDE, but subsequent services operated via Thurso and either Stromness or Quanterness on Orkney on Tuesdays, Thursdays and Saturdays, usually using DH84 Dragons. On 10 September 1936 DH89 G-ADDE, flown by Jimmy Hay, was en route from Aberdeen to Orkney when it force-landed in fog at Mid Backhill Farm near New Byth in Aberdeenshire, fortunately without serious injury to anyone aboard.

Major changes occurred in 1937. On 13 February Aberdeen Airways changed its name to Allied Airways (Gandar Dower) Ltd, and ordered a new DH86B Express four-engined airliner for a proposed new route from Aberdeen to Stavanger in Norway. The share capital of the airline was doubled to £40,000 on 25 March, and on 22 May a proving flight with DH89 G-ADDE was made from Aberdeen to Stavanger, although by then the plans had changed and it was intended to operate the Stavanger service from Newcastle instead of Aberdeen. A proving flight from Newcastle was made on 5 July, and a week later regular flights from Newcastle commenced on the first scheduled service between the UK and

Norway. By the time the service was suspended for the winter on 27 September, the traffic figures had proved disappointing, although the service did resume for the summer of 1938. On 30 November 1937 Allied Airways opened a new Thurso-Inverness service, competing directly with Scottish Airways. The service ran throughout the winter but was suspended on 9 April 1938, and did not operate at all that summer. It was reinstated on 4 November 1938 and operated for a short time during the winter of 1938–9.

In January 1939 the British Government decided that all scheduled air services should be licensed, and on 16 January 1939 the new government body, the Air Transport Licensing Authority (ATLA), began a special four-day sitting in Edinburgh to decide, for once and for all, the extent to which Eric Gandar Dower and E.E. Fresson should be allowed to compete on routes to the Northern Isles. At the beginning of February it announced its findings, namely that:

- Scottish Airways should continue to operate services northwards from Inverness.
- Allied Airways should continue to operate from Aberdeen to Wick, Thurso and Kirkwall.
- The two companies should share the Orkney-Shetland route.
- Allied Airways should be given the rights for the non-stop Aberdeen-Shetland services.
- Scottish Airways should be granted Aberdeen (Dyce)-Inverness-Stornoway rights (the first time it had been allowed to operate from Dyce, and now its only service from Aberdeen). However, no passengers were to be transhipped at Inverness for the Northern Isles, and to make sure of this the two routes were to be deliberately timed to misconnect.
- The two companies should share the Thurso-Kirkwall service (if Scottish Airways wanted to, which was conditional on Thurso opening its own municipal aerodrome).
- No services were to be authorised for Scottish Airways out of Kintore or Dyce to the north of Scotland, and no services were to be authorised for Allied Airways out of Inverness. This was to eliminate 'wasteful competition'.

The ATLA also wanted an undertaking from Allied Airways that its Dyce Aerodrome would be opened to all operators and that efforts to obtain wireless radio facilities would be pursued immediately and before any licences were granted.

An increase in traffic between Aberdeen and the Northern Isles in April 1939 meant that Allied Airways had to duplicate many of its services out of Dyce. It also had to co-operate with Scottish Airways in order to provide services between Orkney and Shetland every day except Sunday, and a twice-daily service between Thurso and Kirkwall. On 10 July 1939 Allied Airways opened a regular, non-stop service between Aberdeen and Shetland on Mondays, Wednesdays and Thursdays. This summer-only schedule was to be the last

Allied Airways Dragon Rapide G-ADAH *Pioneer*, probably in post-war storage at Aberdeen (Dyce). (*L.F. Sarjeant*)

of Mr Gandar Dower's new airline services. During the period 1 January–3 September 1939 the ATLA provided Allied Airways with a subsidy of £3,000 for operating 'lifeline' air services. The first airmail service to North Ronaldsay was operated by Allied Airways DH84 G-ACIT on 31 July, and their summer timetable listed all services as 'Royal Mail Planes'. A special page headed 'Co-operation with Scottish Airways Ltd' showed in detail the shared services.

Upon the outbreak of war on 3 September 1939, operations were suspended.

SCOTTISH MOTOR TRANSPORT/ MIDLAND AND SCOTTISH AIR FERRIES

On 1 June 1932 John Sword, general manager of Western Scottish Motor Transport (Western SMT), persuaded the main board of SMT to set up an aviation department based in Edinburgh and to appoint a commercial manager and flying staff. The first SMT aircraft, DH Fox Moth G-ABWB, arrived at Renfrew, Glasgow, on 2 July. It was joined the following day by another Fox Moth, G-ABWF, and the next day SMT commenced pleasure-flying operations from Edinburgh.

On 9 December 1932 John Sword took the decision to set up his own airline, operating separately from the aviation department of SMT, and placed an order for Airspeed Ferry G-ACBT. This cost £3,975 and his Bentley car was taken in part-exchange to cover £900 of the price. A second Airspeed Ferry was ordered on 18 February 1933, and on 10 March

Mr Sword's new airline was registered as Midland and Scottish Air Ferries Ltd. He remained on the staff of SMT, which continued to operate non-scheduled flights and to expand its fleet.

On 18 April 1933 MSAF launched an experimental air service carrying newspapers from Renfrew Airport, Glasgow, to Campbeltown using DH Fox Moths G-ACCT and G-ACCU. The aircraft landed at Strath Field near Campbeltown, and the service enabled readers there to get their newspapers on the morning of publication. This service became Scotland's first scheduled air service, and on 20 April it was extended to Islay on a trial basis. Initially the shore at Traigh Cill an Rubha, at the head of Loch Indaal, was used, but firmer ground was acquired at Duich Farm, south of Bowmore. This site remained in use until the opening of Glenegedale Airport by Northern and Scottish Airways in 1935. The first official scheduled passengers on the Glasgow-Campbeltown route were carried on 27 April in two Fox Moths, one of which was piloted by Winnie Drinkwater, operating the first regular scheduled air service in Scotland to be commanded by a female pilot. The route extension to Islay was made permanent from 16 May 1933. Two round trips were flown three days each week, and an eight-seat DH Dragon was later used. An 'on demand' stop at Rothesay was added on 24 May 1933, and on 30 May a Renfrew-Belfast (RAF Aldergrove) schedule was inaugurated, with some services operating via Campbeltown. Avro X G-ACGF was used for the special first flight of the service, which was named 'The Irish Scot'. Regular fare-paying services began on 1 June.

Meanwhile, on 19 April 1933 DH Fox Moth G-ACEB of SMT Aviation had paid the first visit to Shetland by a landplane. Piloted by Chief Pilot Bill Caldwell, it carried two officials of the Commercial Bank of Scotland from Edinburgh via Inverness (Longman Fields) and Kirkwall, and landed at Sumburgh Links.

MSAF continued to expand during 1933, opening a Renfrew-Isle of Man (Castletown) route on 12 July. This was intended to connect at the Isle of Man with another new MSAF schedule operating from Liverpool (Speke)-Blackpool (from 9 August)-Isle of Man-Liverpool. Snow and fog at Renfrew during December 1933 resulted in MSAF services using John Sword's new landing ground at Monkton in Ayrshire from 11–23 December, the first recorded continuous use of what was to become Prestwick Airport. During 1933 MSAF carried some 10,000 passengers and was proposing to carry 50,000 in 1934. On 18 January 1934 John Sword announced in the press that he would be linking up the whole of the Western Isles of Scotland and Ireland with continental Europe from March. His services would offer connections at Liverpool for Croydon, to catch Imperial Airways flights to Paris, and from Liverpool it would be possible to connect with KLM services to Amsterdam.

On 9 April 1934 MSAF commenced Renfrew-Liverpool-Romford, Essex, services in co-operation with Romford-based Hillman's Airways. These operated twice daily except on Sundays and were timed to connect at Romford with the Hillman's Airways services to Paris (Le Bourget). The MSAF summer 1934 timetable included twice-daily (except

Sundays) services between Renfrew and Belfast (Aldergrove) via Campbeltown, and a Monday-Saturday service from Renfrew to Islay, again via Campbeltown. In mid-June, however, John Sword received an ultimatum from the directors of SMT, telling him in effect to cease his aviation activities forthwith or leave the group. One of the principal SMT shareholders at the time was the Midland Railway, one of the co-founders of Railway Air Services, who planned to commence Croydon-Birmingham-Liverpool-Belfast-Glasgow air services in August 1934. As a result of the ultimatum John Sword began to wind down his extensive air network. The final MSAF scheduled service was flown from Islay to Renfrew via Campbeltown on 29 September, and the route was taken over by Northern and Scottish Airways on 1 December 1934.

NORTHERN AND SCOTTISH AIRWAYS

Northern and Scottish Airways had its origins in Northern Airways, founded by George Nicholson, a bus operator in Newcastle. From 28 July 1934 the airline operated a Newcastle-Carlisle-Isle of Man service with DH84 Dragon equipment, but following the demise of Midland and Scottish Air Ferries the operating base was transferred to Renfrew Airport, Glasgow, and on 21 November 1934 Northern and Scottish Airways was incorporated 'to operate air services in western Scotland'.

The new airline's first route was inaugurated on 1 December 1934: the former MSAF service from Renfrew to Campbeltown and Islay. The one-way fare from Glasgow to Campbeltown was £30/-/ (!1.50 today) and a further £15/-/ (75p) was charged for the onward leg to Islay. This routeing was later to be split into two separate services. On 17 May 1935 a new route from Renfrew to the Isle of Man was opened, with a fare of £3 5s return.

Six days later, on 23 May, the airline was acquired by the Whitehall Securities Group, owners of United Airways and Spartan Airlines. A working agreement with E.E. Fresson was entered into in June 1935 when his Highland Airways also became part of Whitehall Securities. In August 1937 Northern and Scottish Airways and Highland Airways were merged to become Scottish Airways.

WARTIME OPERATIONS

On the outbreak of war in September 1939, the Scottish internal air routes were initially suspended and National Air Communications status was invoked by the Air Ministry. This immediately placed all airlines and civil airfields and their equipment and personnel at its disposal. Provision was made for retrospective compensation to be paid, although this was to prove a disappointment to most airlines. The suspension of services was short-lived, however, and on 11 September Scottish Airways resumed its services from Renfrew to Campbeltown and Islay. The following day it reinstated the Inverness-Wick-Kirkwall route and the Orkney inter-island services. On 1 November 1939 the service to Kirkwall was extended to Shetland on a charter basis. Allied Airways also restarted operations in mid-September with the exception of the non-stop Aberdeen-Shetland route and the trans-Pentland services.

During the wartime emergency the airline companies were still at the disposal of the armed forces, whose personnel and other 'essential passengers' would get priority for seats. All government passengers would pay the full fares and the airlines' losses would be subsidised, but they were not allowed to make profits amounting to more than 4 per cent of their asset values. Allied Airways managed to negotiate a subsidy of 9d per mile for each ton carried. On 13 October 1939 the Allied Airways aerodrome at Dyce in Aberdeen was requisitioned by the Air Ministry. By then they had only one pilot, Harry Reed, and a few engineers left, but they still managed to maintain services between Dyce, Thurso, Orkney and Shetland. At first both Allied Airways and Scottish Airways used Wideford as the airfield for Kirkwall, as Eric Gandar Dower had closed down his Quanterness airstrip, but on 18 March 1940, a Scottish Airways' DH89 Rapide crashed there, and in late 1941 so did Allied Airways' G-ACZF. When the RNAS airfield at Hatston became operational, both airlines were permitted to use it. In 1942 operations were transferred again, to RAF Grimsetter, the site of the present Kirkwall Airport.

On 6 May 1940 all internal air services came under the jurisdiction of the Associated Airways Joint Committee (AAJC). This had been set up to provide the airlines with a pool of aircraft based at Liverpool, from which they could draw temporary or permanent replacements for losses. Allied Airways did not join the AAJC and so had to make its own arrangements to replace lost or damaged aircraft, but Scottish Airways did come under the AAJC and was able to continue operating throughout the war, carrying more than half of all UK domestic passengers, at load factors of over 80 per cent. The 1940 total of 9,832 passengers was to rise to 12,395 in 1944. On 14 May 1940 the Tiree-Barra-Benbecula-Sollas route was reopened and a new extension to Stornoway was added.

All AAJC operations were suspended during the period 22 May–2 June 1940 to make the aircraft available to fly south and assist in the evacuation of the British Expeditionary Force from Dunkirk. They were withdrawn again for the same purpose on 14 June, but by the end of the month all AAJC services from Renfrew had been restored. When the Allied Airways aircraft returned to Scotland their crews discovered that trenches had been dug across Thurso (Clarendon) and Stromness (Howe) aerodromes to prevent a possible German landing, and airline services were never to be operated from them again.

Both airlines continued operating throughout the war, and in 1945 Allied Airways was flying out of Aberdeen to Wick, Orkney and Shetland, while Scottish Airways served the same destinations from Glasgow and Inverness. Both airlines had standardised on the DH89 Rapide aircraft. On 27 December 1945 Scottish Airways' DH89 G-ACZE suffered considerable damage when an engine failed on take-off from Grimsetter, Orkney.

THE BEA TAKEOVER

The wartime restrictions on civil flying were revoked on 1 January 1946, and on 15 April Scottish Airways restarted full commercial operations on their routes from Renfrew and Inverness to Orkney and Shetland. Their summer timetable also included three round trips from Glasgow to Campbeltown and two direct Glasgow–Islay services, all operated daily except Sunday. The fare from Glasgow to Islay was now £3 1s 6d return.

On 22 August 1946 Railway Air Services, which had been using Dakotas on their main routes from England to Glasgow, brought G–AGZA to Kirkwall to carry out trial operations at Hatston. Flown by E.E. Fresson, the Dakota gave air experience flights to some two dozen Orkney citizens. Dakota services between London (Northolt), Renfrew and Aberdeen (Dyce) by Railway Air Services and Scottish Airways began on 18 November 1946.

From 1 February 1947 the state-owned British European Airways Corporation (BEA) took over UK domestic air services from the private airlines, with the exception of Allied Airways, which technically continued to operate its own services but under contract to BEA. However, on 11 April 1947 it had serviceability problems with all its aircraft and was unable to operate any services that day. BEA issued a statement saying that because Allied Airways had been unable to fulfil its flying programme, BEA's Scottish Division had arranged to operate the Allied Airways routes from the following day. Thus on 12 April BEA took over Allied Airways and one of its DH89 Rapides to maintain continuity of service. For legal purposes BEA was deemed to have officially taken control of Allied Airways on 19 April 1947. Mr Gandar Dower retained ownership of the other three former Allied Airways aircraft, and continued operating them on charter flights from Aberdeen under his own name until early 1950. During the 1960s compensation agreements were reached with the Ministry of Aviation and the Board of Trade, but it was not until 30 May 1973 that BEA finally settled the compensation claims of Mr Gandar Dower regarding the takeover.

CHAPTER TWO

BEA OPERATIONS

The state-owned British European Airways Corporation, generally abbreviated to BEA, was established on 1 August 1946 under the provisions of the 1946 Civil Aviation Act, the other state-owned airlines being the British Overseas Airways Corporation (BOAC) and the British South American Airways Corporation (BSAAC). From that date BEA took over the international routes and the twenty-one Dakotas of the British European Airways Division of BOAC. The Act stated that 'It shall not be lawful for any persons other than the three Corporations and their associates to carry passengers or goods by air … upon any scheduled journey between two places, one of which is in the United Kingdom'. As a consequence, BEA was faced with taking over virtually all UK domestic routes by absorbing the independent airlines currently operating them. This was a task for which it was not yet ready, so for the time being the incumbent airlines continued to operate the services on behalf of BEA. The BEA 1946–7 winter timetable showed the Scottish routes and their temporary operators as follows:

Allied Airways

Aberdeen-Shetland	Daily except Sundays
Aberdeen-Wick-Orkney-Shetland	Daily except Sundays
Aberdeen-Orkney.	Four times each week

All services operated by DH89 Rapide aircraft.

Scottish Airways

Glasgow-Stornoway	Daily except Sundays
Glasgow-Tiree-Barra-Benbecula	Daily except Sundays
Glasgow-Campbeltown	Daily except Sundays

Glasgow-Belfast	Three times each day
Glasgow-Campbeltown-Islay.	Daily except Sundays
Glagow-Orkney-Shetland	Daily except Sundays
Aberdeen-Inverness	Four times each week
Aberdeen-Inverness-Stornoway	Three times each week
Inverness-Wick-Orkney	Twice daily
Wick-Orkney	On demand

All operated by Dakota or DH89 Rapide aircraft.

As part of BEA's re-equipment plan, twenty-five Miles Marathon four-engined aircraft were ordered by the Ministry of Supply on its behalf in late 1946. They were intended to carry fourteen passengers plus freight on the Scottish routes, replacing the DH89 Rapides of Allied Airways and Scottish Airways, and were to be known as the 'Clansman' class. They were to be named after Scottish clans, with the flagship G-AMGW bearing the name *Clansman*. The first production Marathon, G-ALUB, was painted up in BEA livery as *Rob Roy*, and was delivered to Northolt Airport in 1951 for trials on the Highlands and Islands routes. However, the high operating costs of the type when compared to the existing Rapides led to the order being reduced to twelve examples, then to seven, and to the eventual cancellation of the entire order.

In 1947 BEA's UK Division was sub-divided into the English Division, based at Liverpool (Speke), and the Scottish Division, based at Renfrew Airport, Glasgow, and headed by Mr R. McKean. On 1 February it took over the services, staff and aircraft of Scottish Airways, followed by Allied Airways on 12 April. E.E. Fresson, formerly of Scottish Airways, was appointed BEA Manager for Highlands and Islands and transferred to Dyce Airport, Aberdeen, to oversee the takeover of Allied Airways. From 19 May 1947 BEA began using Dakotas on its London (Northolt)-Edinburgh-Aberdeen-Shetland service, the airline's longest domestic route. The journey from Northolt to Aberdeen took 3 hours, at a fare of £15 5s return. The service operated six days a week, and from 2 August the schedules were amended to allow Aberdeen businessmen to spend 6 hours in London and still get home the same day. By then the new Vickers Viking was entering BEA service, but the runway at Aberdeen was considered too short for them, although they were used on services from London to Glasgow and to Prestwick, and also on a relatively short-lived Glasgow-Copenhagen route.

The Junkers Ju52/3 aircraft that BEA inherited from Railway Air Services and Scottish Airways were to have a short service life, initially being relegated from mainline routes to the Scottish internal routes from Glasgow to Inverness and Stornoway and from Aberdeen to Orkney and Shetland. They had been requisitioned from Germany as war reparations and converted to civil standards by Shorts Bros. at Belfast. As they had been constructed to wartime standards for a relatively short service life they were to prove much less reliable than pre-war examples. BEA spent £12,500 on modifying and refurbishing each aircraft, furnishing the passenger cabin in Royal Blue. Ronald Milne recalls flying in one when he was a seventeen-year-old apprentice joiner being sent from Aberdeen to Shetland on a shop-fitting assignment. He remembers that the swastika emblems were still visible beneath the single coat of paint applied by BEA, and that on the outward journey the steward opened a flask of coffee and sold cups of it for 2s 6d each, including a Rich Tea biscuit. On final approach the nose engine was shut down about 5 minutes before touchdown to facilitate landing on the short runway.

The BEA crews found the aircraft easy to fly and light on the controls, with a sedate landing speed of 60mph, but there was always a shortage of good spare parts and for start-up they needed ground power units, which were only kept at Glasgow and Edinburgh. At other airports at least one engine had to be kept running during turn round. If a delay meant this was not possible a ground power unit had to be flown out before the aircraft could depart.

In early 1947, during a service from Kirkwall to Aberdeen, the exhaust pipe on one engine fractured, causing carbon monoxide to seep into the cockpit and almost asphyxiate the crew. After opening the cockpit windows they had to shut down each engine in turn to locate the problem exhaust pipe, eventually making a safe landing at Aberdeen. The Ju52/3s were withdrawn from service on 31 August 1947, but before that the type was used in the relief of the Dubh Artach lighthouse off the west coast of Scotland. Heavy seas had prevented supplies from getting through for several weeks, so Trinity House chartered an aircraft to airdrop provisions. Several passes were made over the islet where the lighthouse was situated – the type's slow-flying abilities making it ideal for the task. The last BEA Ju52/3 movement is believed to have been a non-scheduled flight from Glasgow to Liverpool on 31 August 1947. Captain Fresson of BEA recommended that the type be replaced by sixteen-passenger DH86 biplanes, but in the event the duties were taken over by Dakotas and DH89 Rapides.

During the summer of 1947 BEA's Scottish Division had been scheduling 372 flights each week, but on 6 October the services from Prestwick to London and to Belfast were withdrawn as they were unlikely to prove economical. For the winter season a single daily Dakota service between Shetland and the Scottish mainland replaced several DH89 Rapide flights.

In late 1947 BEA's English Division and Scottish Division were merged back into a single unit. In 1948 the DH89 Rapide was still the mainstay of the local Scottish routes and Lyn Lovie, who was working for BEA around this time, recalls an occasion when Captain Jack Leask, BEA's senior pilot at Aberdeen, took one up for a local test flight after some work had been completed on it. Aboard for the ride were Mr Lovie, a couple of engineers and the BEA Aberdeen Operations Officer, W.S. 'Mac' Love. About 15 minutes into the flight Captain Leask squeezed himself out of the cockpit and handed over control to 'Mac' Love, who, as far as the others on board knew, had never been known to fly anything. However, he handled the aircraft competently and made an excellent landing. Later in his career he was transferred from Aberdeen to become Operations Officer, Berlin.

October 1948 saw the release of the findings of the Douglas Report, produced by Lord Douglas (later to become BEA chairman) at the request of Lord Pakenham, the Minister of Civil Aviation. It was originally not intended for publication, and Lord Douglas's original remit was to examine the operation of sections of the Civil Aviation Act relating to BEA

Associate Agreements. In fact, his report went much further than that and included the following observations on BEA's operations in the Scottish Highlands and Islands:

> The Ministry prepared for me a statement comparing the cost of operating the Scottish services with DH89s by the AAJC in 1944 with the cost of similar services by BEA in 1947/8. This showed that BEA's maintenance costs were three times as high. BEA's explanation that the increase was due mainly to the higher costs of staff, because of the higher wages and shorter hours which now apply, is not very convincing. I suspect the real reason is that their standards of operation are too lavish.

For the winter of 1948–9 the Aberdeen-Edinburgh-London service was suspended as the safety standards at RAF Turnhouse, Edinburgh, were considered inadequate. In January 1949 BEA re-established its Scottish Division, but with less autonomy than before, and during the period January–March 1949 major Dakota maintenance was transferred from Liverpool to Glasgow. In a parliamentary debate on 1 January 1949 Mr Eric Gandar Dower, now an MP, said that air services in Scotland had diminished since nationalisation. Part of the problem was that BEA had reduced the payload of their DH Rapides to five passengers, whereas in his Allied Airways days the type had carried between seven and nine passengers and had thus been able to operate profitably at lower fares. Captain E.E. Fresson was also to complain that BEA did not look after the Rapides sufficiently well, with the result that their payload had to be restricted.

During 15–23 August 1949, the period of the Edinburgh Festival, the prototype Vickers Viscount G-AHRF was loaned to BEA for operation on the London-Edinburgh route, the first ever UK domestic service by a turbo-prop airliner. Another 'first' occurred in February 1950 when, for the first time in British election history, ballot boxes were delivered by air, taken for counting from Shetland to Orkney in a specially-chartered BEA Rapide at a cost of £50. On 28 April BEA opened a new Glasgow-Manchester-Paris route, operated on weekdays by Dakota aircraft. Another new, less-successful service was that from Glasgow to Perth, which commenced on 1 July 1950. It was operated by Rapides daily except Sunday, but was abandoned on 31 August because of poor loads. This may have been because the one daily round trip was flown in the middle of the day, rather than in the morning or evening when it could have connected with trunk services from London.

Many of BEA's Scottish passengers were regulars and had been using the internal routes for many years. On 28 July 1950 Orkney-born Mrs Madeleine McLaren set off from Renfrew on one of her regular visits to Kirkwall. At the time she was ninety-six-years old, and this was her sixth such trip since her ninetieth birthday.

During November 1950, a Benbecula-Renfrew Rapide service under the command of Captain David Barclay encountered severe icing and strong headwinds, forcing the aircraft down to 3,300ft with very little margin for crossing the mountains of Argyll. The flight was eventually completed in 3 hours 6 minutes instead of the usual 1 hour 45 minutes, and with only enough fuel left for another 20 minutes in the air. This experience led Captain Barclay to put forward a strong case for acquiring more sophisticated aircraft with de-icing equipment for the Scottish routes. He had in mind the de Havilland Dove but, after briefly considering the three-engined de Havilland (Australia) Drover, BEA eventually ordered the four-engined de Havilland Heron, which could maintain an altitude of 6,500ft with one engine out and a full load of passengers. It was around this time that BEA decided on a new policy of giving each of their aircraft fleets a class name. The Rapides became the Islander class and the Dakotas, after modification to thirty-two-seat configuration and two-crew operation, became the Pionair class. The Rapides were also modified for single-crew operation, the radio operators being dispensed with.

During the summer of 1951 a seasonal Glasgow-Jersey direct Dakota service was inaugurated, but delays in the delivery of the Pionair conversions left BEA six aircraft short for the summer. As a result, twenty-two services were temporarily pruned from the Scottish area timetable. At this time many BEA stations were quite literally family concerns. At Sumburgh the station superintendent, Mr J. Black, who had worked there since 1936 in pre-BEA days, had but one assistant, his daughter Marie. At Campbeltown Station, Superintendent MacGeachy had been stationed there since 1932, and was also assisted by his daughter in an office in a corner of the local hardware shop. In 1956 they were to be joined by Ella Logan as a traffic clerk on temporary assignment from Islay. She soon became a permanent fixture, and was still to be found there in 1959, opening up the airline section of the shop, making passenger and freight bookings, issuing tickets, making four round trips each day on the airport bus, boarding passengers and completing aircraft load sheets. A similar 'father and daughter' situation existed at Barra.

The February/March edition of Bradshaw's *International Air Guide* (an offshoot of the famous railway timetable publication of the time) showed BEA Dakotas operating Glasgow-Aberdeen-Kirkwall-Sumburgh (Shetland) and back as flights S240A and S204G. The same type also operated flights S212A and S213H Glasgow-Benbecula-Stornoway-Inverness and back on Mondays, Wednesdays and Fridays, and maintained the Renfrew-Belfast schedules. DH89 Rapides operated Aberdeen-Wick-Aberdeen flights S208C and S209J, and a twice-daily round trip from Inverness to Wick and Kirkwall. They also flew from Glasgow to Tiree and back every day except Sunday, with an extension to Benbecula on Mondays, Wednesdays and Fridays. Other Rapide services linked Glasgow with Islay and Campbeltown, and the type also replaced Dakotas on flights S212A/S213H from Glasgow to Benbecula and Stornoway on Thursdays and Saturdays. During March–April 1952 BEA's Vickers Viking maintenance was transferred from Northolt to Renfrew, and during that spring a new Pionair-class Dakota service began from Kirkwall to Manchester via Aberdeen and Edinburgh.

On 30 September 1952 the Islander-class Rapides were withdrawn from all the Scottish routes except that linking Glasgow with Barra. Three examples were retained in Scotland to operate this route and to carry out air ambulance missions. The following day Pionair-class Dakotas took over the former Rapide routes, with some amendments. Tiree was incorporated as a stop on the Glasgow-Benbecula-Stornoway service, and the Glasgow-Campbeltown and Glasgow-Islay routes were combined. A new Pionair Check Three maintenance facility was opened at Renfrew on 13 October 1952.

For the winter of 1952–3 the Aberdeen-Edinburgh Pionair service was extended to Manchester. The type also operated between London and Aberdeen, departing Northolt at 0830hrs, calling at Edinburgh en route and arriving at Dyce at 1310hrs. An eight-day return fare of £11 5s was on offer. On 1 April 1953 an Edinburgh-Birmingham service was introduced, with some flights routeing via Manchester, and on 19 April a Glasgow-Edinburgh-Birmingham-Northolt schedule was inaugurated. Scottish services listed in the July 1953 timetable included:

Glasgow-Guernsey-Jersey   Sunday service
Glasgow-Tiree-Benbecula-Stornoway Weekdays
Glasgow-Campbeltown-Islay   Weekdays
Glasgow-Isle of Man   Fridays
Inverness-Stornoway   Weekdays

(All of the above operated by Pionair aircraft).

Glasgow-Barra   Mondays, Wednesdays and Fridays,
                                 by Islander-class Rapides
Glasgow-Jersey   Saturdays, by Admiral-class Vickers Vikings

The same timetable also gave the addresses of BEA's town offices as:

Aberdeen   BEA Terminal, Joint Station.
Barra   Catherine MacPherson, Post Office, Northbay.
Campbeltown   James MacGeachy, Union Street.
Edinburgh   133 George Street.
Glasgow   122 Vincent Street.
Inverness   Booking Office, Railway Station.
Lerwick   Ganson Bros, Lerwick, and J. Leask and Sons, Lerwick.
Stornoway   BEA Terminal, Cromwell Street.
Wick   82 High Street.

At Glasgow a bus service to the airport was provided from St Enoch Station.

During 1952 BEA had run its own free bus service between Aberdeen and the airport at Dyce, but later a 10s charge was introduced.

On 17 July 1953 the turbo-prop Vickers Viscount began to appear on special flights on the London-Glasgow trunk route. It entered regular service on the route on 2 October 1953 with the inauguration of the 'Clansman' all first-class service. For the summer of 1954 a new Aberdeen-Glasgow-Manchester-London route was introduced.

On 12 February 1955 BEA took delivery of G-ANXA, the first of a pair of Hebrides-class de Havilland Heron 1Bs which were to replace the remaining Rapides. In a ceremony at Glasgow airport on 18 March they were named after Scottish medical pioneers to reflect their intended use on air ambulance flights as well as scheduled services. G-ANXA became *Sir John Hunter* and G-ANXB became *Sir James Simpson*. Scheduled services began on 1 April with a weekday morning schedule from Glasgow to Tiree, replacing the Pionair service which had previously stopped there on its way to Benbecula. The Heron service continued onwards to Barra on three days a week. Flights to Barra landed on the beach at Traigh Mohr, more commonly known as the Cockle Strand, at low tide, and the BEA timetable warned intending passengers to double-check the timings, as they were 'liable to alteration, subject to weather and tide conditions at Barra'.

New pilots were warned to observe the seagulls on the beach before landing, to ensure the birds' knees were still visible. If they were not, the sand was too wet. This did not always prevent mishaps, however. On 30 March 1968 G-ANXA was to get firmly stuck in the wet sand. The aircraft was saved by the resourcefulness of BEA's station superintendent at Barra, Kitty MacPherson, who borrowed a tractor from a local distillery and managed to get the Heron hauled clear of the incoming tide. She was the sole BEA representative on the island, and her duties included reservations, passenger check-in, load control and passing information on the condition of the landing area to incoming flights by two-way radio.

Following delivery of a third Heron, G-AOFY, in time for the 1956 summer season, one aircraft was rostered for the Glasgow-Tiree-Barra service, another was held on standby for air ambulance flights and the third was used on a seasonal service which left Glasgow in the evenings to fly to Inverness and Stornoway. After an overnight stay it departed Stornoway at 0700hrs for Inverness and Glasgow, then flew Glasgow-Inverness-Wick and back during the middle of the day before returning to Stornoway. Robin Mackenzie, then BEA station superintendent at Stornoway, recalls that because of the early morning departure the local hotel was unable to serve crews a cooked breakfast but left out the ingredients for them to

Former BEA Scottish Airways Heron 1B G-ANXB, preserved at the Newark Air Museum, in August 1998.

cook their own. The airport bus departed at 0630hrs, picking up the crew en route. When it arrived at the airport, the sole traffic officer checked in any passengers joining there and completed the load documents. He then assisted the airport firemen in pushing out the Heron and loading baggage while the pilots checked the weather and completed the flight plan. The same traffic officer was on hand to meet the returning aircraft in the evening, and while the crew were away he could process any requests from them for boxes of Stornoway kippers. After dinner in the hotel the crews often visited a local kipper house to watch the curing process and sample a kipper straight from the kiln. The timing of the flights proved popular with Stornoway residents as it enabled them to make day trips to Inverness or Glasgow, and it was repeated for the summer of 1957. John Olive, then a second officer, remembers that on clear days on the Glasgow-Inverness leg the IFR flight plan would be cancelled and the aircraft would be flown visually from Renfrew down the Clyde, across Bute, up Loch Fyne, over the Crinan Canal and the Inner Hebrides and Loch Linhe to Fort William, then via Loch Ness to Inverness, all at a height of 200ft or less, much to the enjoyment of passengers and crew.

The loss of G-AOFY on an air ambulance flight in September 1957 brought about the suspension of this route, as the lost Heron was not replaced.

Meanwhile, an interesting posting for one Heron crew occurred in 1956 when Rolls-Royce Ltd acquired Heron 2D G-AOTI as an executive aircraft. Initially they had no qualified crew for it, so the BEA Heron Flight at Renfrew was approached and Captain Roger Taylor and Second Officer John Olive were loaned to Rolls-Royce. Their first assignment saw them leaving Heathrow for Cologne via Derby and Croydon on 28 September 1956, with Lord Hives and other executives. Further trips took them to Cologne, Geneva and Paris before their detachment ended on 7 October. The BEA Herons were often chartered by the press

BEA Dakota G-AMFV, used on BEA's Scottish network. *(Rod Simpson)*

to fly photographers over ships in trouble in rough seas off the west coast of Scotland, the high winds providing some 'interesting' flying conditions.

Having operated a seasonal Sunday Pionair service from Glasgow to Guernsey in 1955, BEA begun a similar service from Aberdeen via Edinburgh to Jersey in the summer of 1956. However, this was the only Sunday movement at Aberdeen at that time, and the high cost of having the airport opened especially to handle this one movement meant that the service did not survive beyond 1960. During June–August 1956 Pionair maintenance was transferred from Renfrew to London Airport. The Viking fleet had already been withdrawn, so only the Herons were still being looked after at the Glasgow engineering base. 1956 saw visits to Aberdeen and Kirkwall by Viscount turbo-props on route-proving flights, but it would be another six years before the type was used on regular scheduled services to Orkney.

In 1960 Sir John Ure Primrose, a former member of the Air Transport Advisory Council, criticised BEA's Scottish operations, saying that 'BEA's whole set-up in Scotland is ridiculous. They are not operating in the interests of the travelling public. We are only getting what they feel like giving us'. *The Times* newspaper took up the theme, complaining that it was necessary to book a fortnight in advance to secure a seat. Sir John's statement was rejected by Sir Patrick Dollon, chairman of the Scottish Advisory Council on Civil Aviation, who until recently had been a member of the BEA board, saying 'It is a mistake to think that every crofter in the Highlands and Islands can afford to rush about in passenger aircraft'.

Larger aircraft were on the horizon. Series 800 Viscounts were in use on the Glasgow-London trunk route, supplemented by Vickers Vanguards from 20 December 1960, and on 15 December 1959 the Handley Page Herald demonstration aircraft had been tried out in BEA colours at airfields on the Scottish internal network. On 1 April 1961 the Pionairs on the Glasgow-Benbecula-Stornoway route were replaced by Viscounts.

For much of the summer of 1961 BEA services to Edinburgh were disrupted as runway 13/31 was strengthened and resurfaced to enable it to accept Vanguards on the trunk route from London. While this work was in progress BEA's Edinburgh flights were transferred to the airfield at East Fortune, 23 miles from Edinburgh city centre. Preparatory work at East Fortune was carried out by the Ministry of Civil Aviation and BEA at a cost of £40,000, and a former office at BEA's engineering base at London Airport was dismantled, taken by road to East Fortune and re-assembled there as a makeshift passenger terminal. During the four months that East Fortune was in use 2,640 civil aircraft movements and some 96,000 passengers were handled, with aircraft as large as BEA Vanguards passing through.

For the winter of 1961–2 BEA introduced a direct Aberdeen-Sumburgh service on weekdays. In the other direction, on every day except Sundays, Pionair flights from Aberdeen connected at Edinburgh with Vanguard services from Heathrow, and at Glasgow with similar trunk line services operated by Viscounts.

On 10 March 1962 the first of the three Handley Page Heralds ordered on BEA's behalf by the Ministry of Supply and operated by BEA on lease, was delivered. The inaugural service was operated by G-APWB from Glasgow to Sumburgh via Aberdeen, Wick and Kirkwall on 16

April 1962, and the type entered full service from 21 May. The arrival of the Heralds brought to an end BEA Pionair operations in Scotland, the final service being operated by G-ALTT on 19 May 1962 from Islay to Campbeltown and Glasgow as flight BE8679. To mark the occasion, prior to G-ALTT's departure to Islay on the outward leg, all of the types currently in use by BEA in Scotland were lined up on the apron at Renfrew for a 'group photo', comprising a Vanguard, Viscount, Herald, Heron, and of course the last Pionair. Once the full Herald fleet was in service, one example was rostered onto the Glasgow-Campbeltown-Islay route, while the other two operated between Glasgow, Kirkwall and Sumburgh. The Herald was initially considered to be ideal for Highlands and Islands operations, its low-slung fuselage and large freight door enabling baggage and cargo to be handled with the minimum of special equipment. When television first came to Orkney the Heralds flew 8,000 sets from Aberdeen to Kirkwall. Other items of cargo included knitwear and fresh lobsters. However, the economics of operating a fleet of just three examples proved to be the type's undoing in BEA service. An unrealistic passenger load factor of 80 per cent was required just to cover the operating costs, and the airline decided to replace them at the end of the lease with Viscounts, which had already taken over from the Pionairs on the routes to Benbecula and Stornoway. The runways at Kirkwall, Islay and Sumburgh were upgraded, but even when this was done Viscount operations into Sumburgh would still be restricted to a maximum payload of about forty-six passengers because of the difficult approach to the main runway. In the meantime the Heralds soldiered on.

1962 saw major cutbacks to combat losses on the internal Scottish routes. The three-times daily Glasgow-Aberdeen service was reduced to twice daily, and all other internal services were trimmed to one round trip per day. At the beginning of March 1963 it was decided that instead of benefiting from a special subsidy of their own, the Highlands and Islands services would be cross-subsidised by other, profitable BEA routes.

Although they were only destined to serve with BEA for another year or so the Heralds were still very active in 1965, and in that year they began flying to their first destinations outside of Scotland. A 50-minute duration evening service was operated from Glasgow to Belfast, and during the summer peak they were also used for a fortnightly Glasgow-Jersey round trip, with flights BE3738A and BE3739A rostered to take 2 hours 15 minutes in each direction. The final BEA Herald service, flight BE8679 from Islay to Glasgow via Campbeltown, was operated by G-APWB under the command of Captain W.H. Burnett on 31 October 1966. Subsequently, Viscounts took over their services.

On 2 May 1966 the new Abbotsinch Airport at Glasgow began accepting airline services. The first BEA aircraft to land there was actually a Herald on a positioning flight from Renfrew the previous evening. The first commercial flight to land was a chartered BEA Viscount from Edinburgh on 2 May. This was commanded by Captain Eric Starling, BEA's Scottish flight manager, and carried sixty-four members of the staff of Sir Basil Spence Glover & Ferguson, the architects responsible for the design of Abbotsinch. The first scheduled arrival was a BEA Herald from Aberdeen and Edinburgh with forty-one passengers at 0821hrs. A new engineering base was constructed at Abbotsinch, at a cost of over £1m, to take over the minor servicing of

A BEA Herald on take-off. *(Air-Britain)*

Viscounts and Vanguards and all maintenance of the Herons, although this was not ready until 5 October and in the interim the work had mostly to be carried out in the open.

BEA's representative on Islay from the mid-1960s until his transfer to Kirkwall in 1973 was Jack Ridgway, who had begun his BEA career as a traffic clerk at Turnhouse airport, Edinburgh. It was he who suggested to the BEA management that they might want to consider a helicopter service to Islay, along the lines of the one to the Scilly Isles. At that time the Machrie Hotel on Islay was up for sale for around £30,000, complete with golf course, fishing loch and an area of land suitable for helicopter operations. BEA Operations Manager Tom Naylor had confidence in Jack Ridgway's ability to manage the hotel and the helicopter service, but by the time the scheme was approved six months later the hotel had been sold to someone else. The Machrie Hotel had been the site of the first aerial arrival on Islay, when Captain Stirling and Glasgow businessman Robert Paul had landed in an Avro X in July 1928 to have lunch with Duncan McIntyre, the owner of the hotel and estate.

For the summer 1967 season further attempts were made to improve the Scottish schedules. The evening Glasgow-Inverness and early morning Inverness-Glasgow services began to call at Edinburgh, and the late evening Glasgow-Aberdeen flight was extended northward on Mondays, Wednesdays and Fridays to Wick, where it night-stopped before returning south early the next morning. Neither of these innovations generated much extra traffic, however, and they were to be dropped after a couple of seasons. On 1 November 1967 several new BEA divisions, including a Scottish division, came into being, each one a profit centre responsible for the financial success of its own sphere of influence. In 1968 a five-times weekly Manchester-Edinburgh Viscount service was introduced, and from 1 November Viscounts also operated from Inverness to Heathrow via Aberdeen. During the summer of that year the direct Glasgow-Barra service was operated every day of the week, making Barra the first Scottish island to have Sunday air services, an innovation opposed by most of the other islands.

Early in 1969 a series of industrial disputes brought chaos to BEA's Scottish Division's operations. Industrial action by firemen, porters and drivers employed by the airport

BEA Viscount 701 G-AMOP at Glasgow (Renfrew) on 14 June 1961. *(Iain C. Mackay)*

authorities had begun at Glasgow in October 1968 and was to persist intermittently for a year. In January 1969 the firemen at Aberdeen and Edinburgh airports went on strike, closing Aberdeen airport from 15–30 January and Edinburgh airport from 18 January until 3 February. Glasgow airport was also closed during various periods, with flights being diverted to Prestwick. Despite these operational problems, however, the Scottish route network continued to improve. On 8 April 1969 a new passenger terminal at Kirkwall airport was opened by local MP Jo Grimmond, and on 28 April BEA introduced female flight attendants, known as flight clerkesses, on the Scottish internal routes, the first being Isla Roelfina Smith. On 1 December 1969 Captain Eric Starling retired from the post of BEA flight manager, Scotland, but then went on to take charge of BEA's air ambulance operations.

From 1 April 1970 the BEA domestic network, or 'Inter-Britain' network as it was now called, included daily non-stop London-Inverness services. Viscount flight BE5708 arrived at Inverness at 1025hrs and then continued onward to Stornoway, Benbecula and Glasgow. Meanwhile, another Viscount was operating the sectors in reverse order before flying from Inverness to Heathrow in the evening. At Benbecula resources were limited. There were just three staff to handle the flights, no engineers and not even a ground power unit. Because of this, the Viscounts used were fitted with extra batteries to enable them to start up under their own power. The summer of 1970 also saw a number of routes from Glasgow to continental Europe and the Mediterranean being operated via intermediate points, mainly by BEA's Super One-Eleven Division, using BAC One-Eleven series 510 jets which had entered service on routes from Manchester in November 1968. The routes linked Glasgow with Dusseldorf via Manchester, with Malta via Birmingham (using Trident jets), with Palma via Manchester, and with Paris via Birmingham. The Glasgow-Manchester-Palma service was suspended on 25 October 1970 as a direct result of competition from inclusive-tour charter flights.

From 1 April 1971, as the result of yet another BEA reorganisation, ten new divisions were created. Out of the existing Scottish Division, the Scottish Airways Division was formed, responsible for all the Scottish internal services plus the mainline routes from

BEA Viscount 701 G-AMOG at Glasgow (Renfrew) in May 1957. *(Iain C. Mackay)*

Aberdeen and Inverness to London and the Glasgow-Belfast route. R.M. McKean became its director, and a fleet of eight Viscounts (G-AOJB/C/E/F and G-AOHH/I/L/S) plus the two Herons (G-ANXA/B) were allocated to it. Two of the Viscounts were rostered to night-stop at Heathrow to operate the early morning flights to Inverness and Aberdeen, two spent each night at Aberdeen, one at Inverness, and the remainder stayed along with the Herons at Glasgow.

By 1972 the Herons had been in service for nearly twenty years and BEA began to give thought to their possible replacements. The new type would have to have a fixed undercarriage, as the salt spray on the beach at Barra would cause problems with retracting mechanisms, and it would also have to have easy access for stretchers during air ambulance missions. A provisional order was placed for three Britten Norman Trislanders, but a financial crisis at the manufacturer led to the cancellation of this order, and instead BEA purchased two Shorts Skyliners for entry into service in the summer of 1973.

On 1 September 1972 the Scottish Airways Division was incorporated into the British Air Services Division of BEA which had originally been set up to co-ordinate and control the activities of Cambrian Airways and Northeast Airlines, two other subsidiaries. By that time both BEA and its long-haul counterpart, BOAC, were under the overall control of the British Airways Board as part of the process of merging the two airlines into British Airways. During the financial year 1972/3 the Scottish Airways Division made a loss of £750,000. Passenger loads were up by 15 per cent as a result of the North Sea oil boom, but operating costs were kept high by the need to maintain stations at places such as Barra, Benbecula and Tiree, which only handled one or two flights per day. A new engineering and operations block was under construction at Aberdeen to cater for the extra demand for oil-related services, but most of the island airfields still had only basic navigational aids (only Stornoway had an Instrument Landing System). Viscount operations into Sumburgh were still uneconomical

BEA Scottish Shorts Skyliner G-BAIT at Glasgow in 1973. *(Author)*

because of the runway limitations, with hills at each end necessitating a curved approach path, and fog tended to sometimes close the airfield for several days at a time.

On 19 January 1973 tragedy struck when Viscount series 802 G-AOHI was lost with its four crew members whilst on a test flight from Abbotsinch following some maintenance work. During a flight intended to last around 15 minutes the crew proposed to carry out some checks under Visual Flight Rules, although the weather at the time was marginal, with rain, snow and strong winds. The Viscount had climbed to around 4,000ft when it crashed into the side of Ben More, about 35 miles north of Glasgow. The accident was thought to have been caused by the misreading of an altimeter.

At one point during the oil boom, BEA contemplated introducing direct Heron services between Edinburgh and Bergen, but these did not materialise, and on 30 March 1973 G-ANXB operated BEA's last Heron service, from Barra to Glasgow via Tiree. The Heron was replaced on scheduled services by the Shorts Skyliner, a nineteen-seat development of the Skyvan utility aircraft. G-AZYW operated the inaugural service from Glasgow to Tiree as flight BE8746 on 2 April 1973. Later that morning the same machine operated a direct Glasgow–Barra service, and it was to maintain these routes on its own until 20 April when the second example, G-BAIT, arrived at Glasgow. Once both aircraft were in service they also covered the operation of the services from Glasgow to Campbeltown and Islay. The Skyliners also entered service on the Glasgow–Aberdeen and Glasgow–Inverness routes on 1 November 1973, but the type was to be withdrawn in February 1974.

On 1 September 1973 British Air Services began to trade as the British Airways Regional Division. A few days later, on 9 September, two Viscounts on the ground at Edinburgh had to be evacuated after a warning (later found to be a hoax) that there was a bomb on one of them.

On 1 April 1974 BEA finally became fully merged into British Airways.

CHAPTER THREE

LOGANAIR OPERATIONS

During 1961 Capital Services (Aero) Ltd commenced operations, with Captain Duncan McIntosh flying its sole Piper Apache on a variety of charter services. Among these were flights for the Logan Construction Company, which led to a decision by that company to set up its own in-house flying operation. The new venture was formed as Loganair on 1 February 1962, and Captain McIntosh left Capital Services (Aero) to become Loganair's manager/chief pilot. The initial base was at Edinburgh Airport, but operations were soon transferred to Renfrew Airport, Glasgow. A Piper Aztec was acquired, followed in 1963 by a further example and Piper Tri-Pacer G-ARHV. The second Aztec allowed Loganair to take on work for companies other than its parent, and the Tri-Pacer was used for crew transfers, training and aerial photography.

During 1963 Captains Ken Foster and Lynn John joined Loganair to carry out most of the external charters, and it was in that year that Willie Logan of the Logan Construction Company used a Loganair aircraft to fly into Dundee Airport with his company's successful tender for the new Forth Road Bridge, arriving with the documents 15 minutes before the deadline. An early Loganair customer was the Army, which used aircraft to transport mail, food and other supplies to the radar station on remote St Kilda, whose native population had been evacuated at their own request, the last leaving in 1930. There was no suitable landing area, so the supplies had to be dropped from very low level onto the main island of Hirta. Other notable early contracts included one from Littlewoods Pools to fly football pools coupons from Renfrew to Belfast from 1963–5, and from Belfast to Liverpool in 1966.

In late 1963 Loganair inaugurated its first regular passenger service. This was a charter service, operated in conjunction with Mackay Bros (Dundee) Ltd and under a dispensation from the Ministry of Aviation, between Dundee and Edinburgh to connect with BEA's 0750hrs service from Edinburgh to Heathrow. The fare varied according to the number of passengers carried. If all five seats were filled the one-way fare was £1 10s, or a single passenger could charter the whole Aztec for £15 return.

During 1964 Loganair was awarded a charter contract to fly newspapers from Glasgow to Stornoway, enabling them to go on sale on Lewis before the arrival of BEA's scheduled service. The Aztec used was then available to carry cargo only on the otherwise empty leg back to Glasgow, and the islanders took advantage of this to transport fresh lobsters and Harris Tweed cloth to the mainland. The charter licence was later varied to include Benecula, and the NAAFI there used the service to bring over fresh milk and vegetables for the Army garrison. Loganair tried many times to obtain permission to carry passengers on the return leg to Glasgow, but these applications were bitterly and successfully opposed by BEA on the grounds that the corporation had lost £5 million on its Highlands and Islands services over the previous eighteen years and could not afford any competition. Eventually, Loganair was permitted to carry a maximum of fifteen passengers each week on the Stornoway-Glasgow leg and this contract was to continue until 1974, when BEA finally amended its schedules to include a morning Glasgow-Stornoway service.

On 23 January 1966 Willie Logan needed to fly from Edinburgh to Inverness on business but the Loganair fleet was fully committed, so he chartered an Aztec from Strathallan Air Services. On the approach to Inverness the aircraft crashed into Craig Dunain and Loganair's founder was killed. During 1966 Loganair became a limited company. Flying for the Logan Construction Company was diminishing, so plans were laid for a revival of the Orkney inter-island services last operated by Highland Airways in the 1930s. Central to these plans was the new Britten Norman Islander feeder aircraft, whose development was being studied closely. In the meantime Loganair commenced scheduled services on the Glasgow-Oban-Mull route, and made a small piece of airline history on 1 May 1966. A Cherokee Six aircraft was being flown on behalf of the Ministry of Aviation to check the landing lights at the new Glasgow airport at Abbotsinch. The aircraft made a low pass along the runway and then touched down, making Loganair the first operator to land there.

On 16 June 1967 the first Loganair air ambulance flight was operated from Oronsay to Glasgow by Aztec G-ASYB. This type of flying was to become a Loganair speciality in the coming years.

In July 1967 the first production Britten Norman Islander G-ATWU was delivered to Loganair on a short-term lease for crew training and route-proving trials. In August this machine was replaced by the fourth production example, G-AVKC, which was taken to Orkney by Captain Jim Lee, Loganair's first resident pilot there. That month Loganair became the first airline in the world to operate the Islander when it revived the pre-war Orkney inter-island services with routes linking Kirkwall with Stronsay, Sanday, North Ronaldsay, Westray and Papa Westray. Seventy passengers were carried during the first week, the services being operated under an arrangement with the Orkney Islands Shipping Company, which enabled government aid for the steamship services also to be made available to Loganair. This involvement was to last until 1977.

During 1968 a contract was awarded by the Post Office for the carriage of computer punched cards from Glasgow to Blackpool for processing overnight on the Premium Bonds computer 'ERNIE' at Lytham St Annes. The processed cards were then flown north again the following morning. On 8 October 1968 the share capital of Loganair was acquired by the National Commercial Bank of Scotland, which was to merge with the Royal Bank of Scotland the following year. John Burke, the managing director of the Royal Bank of Scotland, then became chairman of Loganair, and Captain McIntosh became managing director. In October 1968 Beech 18 G-ASUG was acquired from BKS Air Survey. Although used on some scheduled services it was fitted out as an executive charter aircraft until its retirement in 1975. It is still preserved in Loganair colours at the Museum of Flight at East Fortune in Scotland.

Further new equipment arrived on 3 March 1969 in the shape of Shorts Skyvan G-AWYG. This turbo-prop feeder-liner could hold up to eighteen people but was expensive to operate, and on longer stages its capacity was limited to twelve to fifteen passengers. It was to be phased out five years later. On 14 July 1969 Loganair inaugurated its first international scheduled service, from Glasgow via Aberdeen to Stavanger in Norway. The first trip was operated by the Beech 18 in a six-seat layout, but on occasions the Skyvan was used, configured for fourteen passengers. Although the flights originated in Glasgow, the bulk of

Beech 18 G-ASUG at the Museum of Flight at East Fortune in 1992, after its retirement from Loganair service. *(Author)*

Loganair Shorts Skyvan G-AWYG served with them for five years. *(Air-Britain)*

the traffic was between Aberdeen and Stavanger and around 90 per cent of the passengers were Norwegians. During December 1969 the load factor between Aberdeen and Stavanger was around 40 per cent and the service was making a small loss. It was suspended on 4 November 1970 because of continuing poor passenger figures.

In May 1970 Loganair operated its first Shetland scheduled service, from Sumburgh to Unst. The airfield at Baltasound on Unst is the most northerly in the British Isles, and the lighthouse at Muckle Flugga, a rock off the northern tip of Unst, is the northernmost inhabited point in the UK. Unst is a breeding ground for the Great Skua, making it a place of special interest to ornithologists. The airstrip was constructed by the Army in 1968 as part of the OPMAC (Operation Military Aid to the Community) scheme. Other airstrips constructed under this scheme included Glenforsa on Mull, which was the first to be built under the scheme in 1966, and Breakish on Skye. During 1969–70 Loganair carried out trial flights to other Shetland outer islands, including Foula, Papa Stour and Fetlar, to determine their suitability for scheduled services and air ambulance missions.

Back on the Scottish mainland, Loganair made a return to Dundee in 1970, this time with a service to Glasgow (Renfrew). The airfield at Riverside Park, Dundee, was initially unusable due to waterlogging, and the Islander aircraft had to use RAF Leuchars on the other side of the River Tay. After a slow start, passenger loads doubled when Riverside Park became available again

Loganair Jetstream 31 G-LOGU at Sumburgh in June 1994. *(Kieran Murray)*

in August 1971, and the twice-daily service was increased to three rotations each day. The Skyvan and, later, Britten Norman Trislanders were also used, but the service required a subsidy to keep fares acceptably low, and when this was withdrawn in 1975 the service was dropped.

Loganair's revenues were unexpectedly boosted in January 1971 when an RAF Blackburn Beverley heavy transport aircraft, bound for Unst with radar equipment for installation at Saxa Vord, elected to land at Sumburgh instead. Loganair Islanders ferried the cargo to Unst in eleven trips, with the Skyvan also being used to carry the bulkier items.

During 1971 two new airfields were opened, one on Shetland and one on Orkney. The Shetland airport at Sumburgh, on Shetland's southern tip, was often subject to fog and was a 25-mile road journey from the principal town of Lerwick. With the aid of the Royal Engineers a new airfield was constructed at Tingwall, only two miles away. A rocky hump was blown up and STOLMAT plastic matting laid. Inter-island services commenced on 15 November 1971 and the new airfield was an immediate success. In May 1971 a new airstrip at Eday on Orkney was opened and passenger services began. Because of its proximity to Eday's Bay of London the new airfield was named London Airport – not to be confused with other airfields with a similar name!

In 1972 the seasonal Glagow-Oban-Mull weekend route was reopened, this time with an extension to Coll and Tiree. Scheduled services through Fetlar commenced in May, an

Loganair Islander G-AXKB at Kirkwall in April 1976. *(L.F. Sarjeant)*

Aberdeen-Inverness route opened on 2 July, and on 24 November the first trial landing was made at Longhope, near Hoy in Orkney. Scheduled services to Hoy began on 16 October 1973.

Loganair had been operating air ambulance flights in a supplementary capacity to BEA since 1967, and on 1 April 1973 the airline assumed full responsibility for all Scottish Air Ambulance services under a contract from the Scottish Home and Health Department. Scheduled services to Whalsay on Shetland were launched during the autumn of 1973, and on 19 December Captain Alan Whitfield carried out Loganair's first landing on the Out Skerries, in Islander G-AXSS. After initial use for air ambulance flights, the airfield opened for scheduled services in the spring of 1974.

By 1973 the oil exploration activity in the waters around Shetland was making itself felt in terms of increased air travel to and from the Scottish mainland. In anticipation of increased charter work Loganair had taken delivery of its first Britten Norman Trislander aircraft in July and, following the award of its first oil-related contract from Shell in December, a Trislander was based at Sumburgh for operations to and from Aberdeen. This contract was lost to Dan-Air in 1974, but alternative work was found for the Trislander in October when Loganair began operating the Glasgow-Tiree-Barra route on behalf of BEA, and then took over the route in its own right in the spring of 1975. Loganair moved its oil-support base to Aberdeen in March 1975 and based two Trislanders there.

Loganair Islander G-AXKB at Kirkwall in April 1976. *(L.F. Sarjeant)*

During 1975 an Inverness-Edinburgh scheduled service was launched, and a Stornoway-Benbecula-Barra Islander operation was inaugurated on 1 October. The handover of British Airways' 'thinner' Scottish routes to Loganair would continue in 1976 with the transfer of the Inverness-Wick-Kirkwall service on 1 April. In the meantime there were problems at Tingwall. The temporary licence for the airstrip was not renewed in October 1975 and services were suspended until a new airstrip was constructed a little further up the valley. This was commissioned by the Shetland Islands Council and featured a fully lit, hard-surfaced 760-metre runway, fire cover, fuel and radio facilities, a small terminal building and a hangar. The first trial landing was made in July 1976 and the new airfield was licensed for scheduled services on 20 October. Fair Isle was added to the Shetland network on 7 June 1976.

On 11 January 1977 the new oil terminal at Flotta on Orkney was opened, and on 1 March Loganair inaugurated scheduled services from Kirkwall to Flotta via Hoy, using Islanders. However, by 1981 the stop at Hoy had been discontinued because of the boggy conditions there and the Flotta service was ended when Occidental Oil started providing a free sea ferry service. During 1977 Loganair received its first Twin Otter aircraft, a type ordered specifically for oil-related charter work. At the height of the oil boom the airline was to have seven Twin Otters and three Trislanders based at Aberdeen for charter work, principally for Chevron Oil. Most flights were between Aberdeen and Unst in support of the Ninian oil field. Later, Chevron invited tenders for the contract based on the use

Loganair Trislander G-BAXD at Inverness on 23 March 1975. *(L.F. Sarjeant)*

of larger, four-engined DHC-7 aircraft. Loganair placed an order for one example and submitted its tender, but the contract was awarded to Brymon Airways. The DHC-7 order was cancelled, and Loganair was obliged to find other work for its Twin Otters on the scheduled service network.

On 1 April 1977 Loganair began operating the former British Airways service from Glasgow to Campbeltown and Islay. In place of a once-daily Viscount service to both places, Loganair introduced separate Trislander flights to each destination on a twice-daily basis, making day trips possible. On 9 July 1978 a Shorts 330 aircraft was used to inaugurate a Scottish Airports-sponsored service linking Prestwick with Aberdeen and Edinburgh. The service was timed to connect with trans-Atlantic flights at Prestwick, and during the 1979 season (July–November) around 4,000 passengers were carried. The service was resumed on 28 April 1980, but far fewer passengers were carried that summer. This resulted in a loss to Loganair and a consequently higher subsidy per passenger from the BAA, so it was decided, reluctantly, to discontinue the service.

On 2 April 1979 Loganair inaugurated its longest non-stop route within Scotland, from Edinburgh to Tingwall, a flight of some 2 hours' duration. The first service was flown by Captain Whitfield, using Twin Otter G-RBLA in an eighteen-seat configuration. Twin Otters were also used to run seasonal services from Glasgow to Londonderry and to Enniskillen, and in 1981 the Edinburgh-Tingwall service was extended to Unst. On 15 May 1979

Trislander G-BCYC was damaged beyond repair in an incident at Aberdeen, fortunately without fatalities. During 1979 Loganair claimed the distinction of being the first airline to introduce a complete ban on in-flight smoking. The fleet in 1979 comprised seven Islanders, seven Twin Otters and one Shorts 330. Loganair was operating over 670 scheduled service flights each week to thirty-one destinations.

In February 1980 Islander G-BFCX came to grief whilst landing at Rousay in wet and windy conditions, and ended up in a ditch. The airstrip had only just been opened and it was intended for use on air ambulance sorties, but as a result of this incident it was declared unsuitable. The unfortunate Islander was airlifted to Kirkwall under a Bristow's S-61 helicopter for repair. During the year Loganair dropped Sumburgh from its route network, blaming high airport charges. The Shetland operating base was then transferred to Tingwall. Oil support charter operations continued, and Bandeirante turbo-prop aircraft were acquired specifically for this purpose in 1980. However, during the financial year 1980/1 a loss of £700,000 was incurred, and further heavy losses occurred during 1981/2 (£1 million) and 1982/3 (£350,000), reflecting the loss of the Chevron Oil contract and the cost of upgrading the fleet.

The scheduled service network continued to develop, with new routes being introduced and equipment being upgraded. In April 1980 Loganair took over the Edinburgh-Belfast

Loganair Trislander G-BCYC was damaged beyond repair at Aberdeen on 15 May 1979. (Air-Britain)

Loganair Jetstream 41 G-LOGK at Sumburgh. *(Kieran Murray)*

Loganair Twin Otter G-RBLA at Inverness on 15 March 1980. *(L.F. Sarjeant)*

Loganair Islander G-AYXK at Glasgow in 1975. *(Author)*

route from British Airways, using Shorts 330s. The same type was also used to inaugurate an Edinburgh-Kirkwall route in 1980, with a stop at Wick being incorporated the following year. Over the years, Twin Otter, Shorts 360 and ATP aircraft were utilised on this service. For the summer of 1980 Loganair took over the former Dan-Air weekend service from Prestwick to the Isle of Man. This was to be operated for four summer seasons. In 1981 a twice-daily Glasgow-Belfast Shorts 330 route was launched, as well as a Belfast-Blackpool service, Loganair's first route to England. On 16 October 1981 an Aberdeen-Inverness-Glasgow Twin Otter service was introduced, although the Aberdeen-Inverness leg was to be dropped from 15 April 1982. Ten days later the Trislanders, on the services from Glasgow to Campbeltown and Islay, were replaced by Twin Otters, occasionally supplemented by Islanders and Bandeirantes. The Trislanders were used to replace Islanders on Barra-Benbecula-Stornoway services, and Twin Otters were placed on the Glasgow-Barra route. Loganair was the sole operator at Barra, providing all airport services there, including the fire tender and the terminal building which had been opened in June 1978.

In October 1982 the British Airways Edinburgh-Manchester route was taken over. Shorts 330s were used initially, followed by Shorts 360s in 1983, and from November 1983 by a forty-four-seat Fokker F-27 leased from British Midland Airways. When this was involved in an accident at Manchester on 11 January 1984, a seventy-six-seat Viscount was leased from

Loganair Islander G–BFNV at Inverness on 5 April 1983. *(L.F. Sarjeant)*

Loganair Bandeirante G–BIBE gets airborne from Inverness on 6 September 1981. *(L.F. Sarjeant)*

British Air Ferries. Named *The Flying Scotsman*, this aircraft maintained services on the route while the F-27 was being repaired.

On 7 February 1983 the Shorts Aerospace Company opened its factory airfield at Sydenham, Belfast, to scheduled airline services. It was initially known as Belfast Harbour Airport, later changed to Belfast City Airport. Loganair transferred its Belfast services to this much more centrally located airport on 21 November 1983, and soon experienced an increase in Belfast passenger loads of up to 40 per cent as a result. With effect from 2 December 1983, control of Loganair passed from the Royal Bank of Scotland to British Midland Airways. Loganair Financial Director Scott Grier acquired a 25 per cent shareholding and became managing director, succeeding Captain Duncan McIntosh, who retired from Loganair after a twenty-one-year career which included the awarding of the OBE in 1976 for his services to the people of the Highlands and islands of Scotland.

In December 1983 the Loganair fleet comprised one Fokker F-27 series 100, one Shorts 360, two Bandeirantes, five Twin Otters and six Islanders. One of the last named was lost on 1 June 1984 when G-BDVW overshot on landing at Sanday and was written off. In October 1984, Glasgow-Manchester service BDVW overshot on landing at Sanday and was written off. In October 1984 Glasgow-Manchester services were launched using the Fokker F-27, but that same month saw the closure of the Aberdeen base, as Loganair had been denied traffic rights for an Aberdeen-Shetland scheduled service and had take the decision to withdraw

Loganair Bandeirante G-BIBE taxiing at Inverness on 6 September 1981. *(L.F. Sarjeant)*

Loganair Shorts 330 G-BIRN at Edinburgh on 1 October 1983 with a Britannia Airways 737 taxiing past. *(L.F. Sarjeant)*

from oil support charter work. The Bandeirantes were redeployed onto Glasgow-Belfast and Edinburgh-Inverness scheduled service flights.

During the mid-1980s Loganair became interested in developing regional routes to continental Europe under the British Airways 'largesse' scheme. This scheme came about as the result of a review of UK civil aviation policy by the Civil Aviation Authority, which led to a government White Paper. The CAA's recommendation that British Airways' international networks from UK provincial cities should be hived off and handed to the independent airlines was turned down. Instead, the smaller airlines (with the exception of British Caledonian Airways) were to be encouraged to open routes from the provincial airports. British Airways was to offer them financial assistance with their development costs to the tune of £450,000 per new route, spread over three years. The offer covered up to fifteen new routes from the six regional airports specified, whether they were completely new routes or ones which British Airways was already operating. Loganair considered routes to Brussels, Cologne, Copenhagen and Rotterdam, and evaluated the Dornier 228 as a potential replacement for the Twin Otters. It would have reduced the Edinburgh-Tingwall flying time from 2½ hours to 1 hour 25 minutes, but it was unpressurised and thus considered unattractive for routes to mainland Europe. The

Jetstream 31 was also considered, but did not posses the short take-off and landing capability needed on many island routes. In the end, the launch of international services was put on hold for the immediate future.

By 1986 Loganair was holding several Post Office mail contracts. One Twin Otter operated Aberdeen-Glasgow-Liverpool-Glasgow, while another flew Edinburgh-Liverpool and return. Shorts 360s were used between Glasgow and the East Midlands, Glasgow and Luton, Belfast and Luton, and Edinburgh and Luton.

On 12 June 1986 Twin Otter G-BGPC was operating a scheduled Glasgow-Islay service with fourteen passengers aboard. Approaching Islay in conditions of low cloud and heavy drizzle, both pilots misidentified Laphroaig on Islay as Port Ellen. Shortly after turning inland near Laphroaig the aircraft struck rising ground, which was obscured in hill fog at 360ft above mean sea level. Captain Christopher Brookes was killed and co-pilot David Isley sustained severe injuries, although the passengers escaped with minor injuries and shock.

In 1987 the engineering base at Glasgow employed sixty-eight staff. Engineers were also out-stationed at Edinburgh (nine), Belfast (five), Kirkwall (three), Stornoway (two) and one each at Lerwick and Manchester. An extract from the summer 1987 timetable showed the following service frequencies:

Loganair Twin Otter G-BGPC was lost in a fatal crash on Islay on 12 June 1986. (Air-Britain)

Glasgow–Londonderry	One weekday rotation plus weekend services
Glasgow–Campbeltown	Two weekday rotations
Glasgow–Islay	Two weekday rotations
Glasgow–Skye	One rotation on four days each week
Glasgow–Tiree–Barra	One daily rotation
Stornoway–Benbecula	One daily rotation, extended to Barra on most days
Edinburgh–Wick–Kirkwall	One rotation on six days each week
Inverness–Glasgow	One rotation each weekday
Kirkwall–Wick–Inverness	Two weekday rotations plus one on Saturdays
Belfast–Manchester	Two weekday rotations plus extras on some weekdays and one on Saturdays
Edinburgh–Manchester	Five weekday rotations plus one on Sundays
Belfast–Blackpool	Daily rotation plus extra on Saturdays
Londonderry–Isle of Man and Londonderry–Blackpool	Saturday rotations
Tingwall–Fair Isle	Single rotation on three days each week
Kirkwall–Fair Isle	Saturday rotation
Tingwall–Whalsay–Fetlar–Unst	One rotation each weekday
Plus the Orkney Internal air service	

One of Loganair's most frequent flyers at this time was Miss Maisie Muir, who for the past seventeen years had been operating the North Isles banking service for the Royal Bank of Scotland. By 1987 she had flown over 9,000 sectors on this business. A typical working week for her involved the following itinerary:

Monday	Kirkwall–Eday (or North Ronaldsay)–Kirkwall
Tuesday	Kirkwall–Sanday (or, once a month, Papa Westray)–Kirkwall
Wednesday	Kirkwall–Westray–Kirkwall
Thursday	Kirkwall–Stronsay–Kirkwall
Friday	Kirkwall–Westray–Kirkwall

In December 1987 Loganair became a subsidiary of the Airlines of Britain Group, the parent company of British Midland Airways.

During 1988 and 1989 two BAe 146 series 200 jets were acquired with the intention of using them to open new routes to the Channel Islands and mainland Europe. In the event, however, they were mainly used on services from Manchester to Belfast, with occasional use on other trunk routes such as Edinburgh–Manchester and on summer schedules to the Channel Islands. Both machines were traded in to British Aerospace as part-payment for ATP turbo-props, but G-OLCB was leased back again during March–April 1992 for use by the Prime Minister in the General Election campaign. Another jet type to be used briefly was the BAC One-Eleven. Series 500 aircraft G–AZUK and G–BNIH were leased from Ryanair during 1988 and 1989 and were mainly used on the Edinburgh-Manchester route.

For the summer of 1992 new turbo-prop equipment in the form of Jetstream 31s and ATPs was in service on routes from Edinburgh and Glasgow to Southampton, from Glasgow to Leeds-Bradford, from Manchester to Knock and to Londonderry, and from Glasgow to Bergen via Kirkwall. By 1993 larger Jetstream 41s had been introduced and were operating between Kirkwall and Bergen.

In March 1994 a reorganisation of the British Midland group of companies led to the Loganair cross-border routes to England being transferred to Manx Airlines (Europe), another British Midland subsidiary. Along with the routes went eight ATPs and three Jetstream 41 aircraft. In return, Loganair received three Shorts 360s to add to the five already being operated. At that time a team led by Managing Director Scott Grier was attempting to put together a management buy-out of the airline, which had not been profitable for three years. British Airways had expressed an interest in franchising out its Highlands and Islands services, and an agreement was signed on 11 July 1994 which resulted in Loganair becoming the first British Airways franchise operator, the agreement to take effect from 1 August. The Loganair fleet was repainted in British Airways colours, with the exception of the Islanders used on air ambulance flights. As well as operating Scottish routes on behalf of British Airways, Loganair continued to operate its own inter-island schedules in Orkney and Shetland.

On 1 September 1996 the Airlines of Britain Group created British Regional Airlines by merging Loganair and Manx Airlines (Europe). This arrangement only lasted until 28 February 1997 when the long-planned management buy-out took place and Loganair became independent once more, operating its own inter-island services and the British Airways franchised routes. On 10 June 1997 Loganair Islander G-BLDV was used to unveil one of the new British Airways 'World Images' tail designs at Glasgow Airport. In October

Loganair BAe 146 G-OLCB. The type was mainly used on services out of Manchester. *(Air-Britain)*

1998 Loganair took over the British Airways routes linking Sumburgh with Kirkwall, Wick, Inverness and Edinburgh, and even began competing with British Airways for a while on the Glasgow-Sumburgh route. Saab 340 turbo-props were acquired and used to upgrade the equipment on the Glasgow-Kirkwall and Edinburgh-Kirkwall routes in July and August 1999, and in 2000 the Stornoway-Inverness route was taken over from British Regional Airlines.

On 27 February 2001 Loganair suffered another fatal accident. Shorts 360 G-BNMT was rostered to operate Royal Mail charter flight 670A from Edinburgh to Belfast. The aircraft had landed at Edinburgh at 0003hrs and had been parked in conditions of moderate snowfall. After spending the day on the ramp at Edinburgh the aircraft encountered problems with

Loganair Trislander G-BDDS at Islay on arrival from Glasgow in 1977. *(Author)*

Loganair Jetstream 31 G-LOGC on display at the 1992 Prestwick Air Show.

engine start-up, but eventually took off for Belfast at around 1730hrs. During the initial climb a double engine failure occurred and both crew members were killed when the aircraft came down in the Firth of Forth some 100m from the shoreline near Granton Harbour. The accident investigation determined that the engine failures were caused by an undetected accumulation of ice and snow during the period the aircraft was parked.

On 15 September 2001 the British Airways franchise for the Aberdeen-Kirkwall route was taken over from British Regional Airlines, with Saab 340 aircraft being utilised.

In 2003 the Orkney inter-island operation was being managed by Christine Allen, then in her twenty-ninth year of service with Loganair. Six times every weekday, and four times on Saturday, an Islander left Kirkwall for the outer islands, most services calling at two islands before returning. The most distant of these islands, North Ronaldsay, is 33 miles away from Kirkwall, while the nearest is Stronsay at 16 miles. No sector takes more than 15 minutes and Loganair holds the record for the world's shortest fixed-wing scheduled air service, the leg between Westray and Papa Westray. The flights are scheduled to take 2 minutes for the 1.3-mile journey, but Captain Alsop once managed it in 58 seconds. On a clear day the windsock at the other airfield can easily be seen from the departure airstrip. Two Islanders were also based at Tingwall in Shetland, one for the outer island schedules and one on standby for air ambulance flights.

2004 was another year of expansion for Loganair. On 1 March seven British Airways routes were taken over from British Airways CitiExpress. These were Edinburgh-Belfast, Aberdeen-Sumburgh, and routes from Glasgow to Belfast, Benbecula, Stornoway, the Isle of Man and Aberdeen. Four sixty-six-seat ATP aircraft were wet-leased for twelve months to operate these services whilst various aircraft types were evaluated as replacements. On 2 May a Glasgow-Galway service was introduced on six days each week, and the following day a weekday Edinburgh-Isle of Man route was opened. Thirty-four-seat Saab 340s were used on both routes. In May 2005 Loganair announced that it had secured the rights to operate Derry-Dublin and Knock-Dublin services for a three-year period from 22 July 2005 under Public Service Obligation (PSO) contracts from the Irish Government. The Derry-Dublin route was the first to be funded under a PSO contract by the Irish Government, although Loganair had in fact been operating a double daily service for the past four years as a private initiative. Following the withdrawal of Aer Arran from the Derry-Manchester route, Loganair also took over that service from 22 July 2005. However, it was to be withdrawn in January 2006. Daily services between Dublin and Glasgow commenced under another British Airways franchise arrangement on 10 August 2005.

In 2006 Loganair lost the contract for the provision of air ambulance services to the Northern Isles. This led to a requirement for re-tendering for the scheduled passenger services, and although Loganair continued to serve the Orkney outer islands, the Shetland services from Tingwall to Fair Isle, Foula, Papa Stour and the Skerries were transferred to Directflight on 1 August 2006. Loganair had been operating these routes for thirty-seven years, and before leaving them a farewell tour around the islands took place on 24 July 2006. On board the Islander were Loganair Chairman Scott Grier, Director of Flight Operations Gordon Young and former pilot Alan Whitfield, who had operated the first service into Foula

Loganair Twin Otter G-BIEM at Glasgow on a rainy day in September 1989. *(Author)*

on 12 November 1969. The pilot for the special flight was Eddie Watt, who had flown the route for the past ten years. Many of the islanders expressed regret over the loss of Loganair, with all its accumulated route experience, and had doubts about the ability of Directflight to provide as good a service on such a challenging route network. Some Loganair staff, including pilot Marshall Wishart, were taken on by Directflight, but Eddie Watt remained with Loganair, being retrained onto the Saab 340 and deployed on the Aberdeen-Sumburgh route.

From 11 December 2006 all Orkney inter-island services went onto a 'payment at time of booking' basis, intended to reduce the number of costly 'no-shows' for flights. The tickets were still changeable or refundable, but only if 24-hours notice was given. Looking to the future, Loganair has been awarded new PSO contracts by the Scottish Executive, which cover services from Glasgow to Barra, Campbeltown and Tiree until at least 31 March 2009. These contracts come under the provisions of the Highlands and Islands Air Services (Scotland) Act of 1980, which makes subsidies available to meet deficits incurred in providing socially necessary 'lifeline' air services to the Scottish Highlands and Islands. In the summer of 2007 a new Islander service between Kirkwall, North Ronaldsay and Fair Isle was introduced, providing a link between the major bird-watching centres on Fair Isle and North Ronaldsay, as well as improving access to Fair Isle from the mainland.

On 14 January 2008, Loganair and Flybe announced the signing of a franchise agreement, to take effect from 26 October 2008, following the termination of Loganair's franchise agreement with British Airways. Under the new contract, Loganair aircraft will be repainted in Flybe colours, and the Flybe low-fares range will be extended to cover the Highlands and Islands network.

In March 2008, Loganair announced its return to Dundee airport. From 21 May 2008, the airline was due to operate three round trips each weekday between Dundee and Birmingham, with a single rotation on Sundays, and one weekday round trip between Dundee and Belfast City Airport.

CHAPTER FOUR

BRITISH AIRWAYS (AND FRANCHISE OPERATORS) OPERATIONS

On 29 May 1974 Viscount 802 G-AOHO operated the regular British Airways scheduled service between Inverness and Kirkwall on the fortieth anniversary of the first airmail service over the route, flown by Captain E.E. Fresson's Highland Airways. The Viscounts were also used for occasional Kirkwall-Bergen charter flights, but on the Aberdeen-Sumburgh route the seventy-one-seat aircraft were restricted to a maximum load of forty-five passengers, and a £2 million order had been placed for two HS748 series 2As as their replacement. In forty-four-seat configuration the 748s would be able to carry a full payload into Sumburgh, and also use the crosswind runway there if necessary. The first example, G-BCOE 'Glen Livet', was delivered on 10 July 1975, but prior to that a new Viscount service between Aberdeen and Manchester was inaugurated on 27 October 1974, and it was to be several years before the last Viscounts were finally retired. The inaugural HS748 service was operated by G-BCOE on the Glasgow-Aberdeen-Kirkwall-Sumburgh route on 4 August 1975, and from then until 1982 the twin turbo-prop aircraft operated alongside the Viscounts on Scottish routes.

In April 1978 British Airways launched direct services from Glasgow to Paris, Milan (via Birmingham) and Copenhagen. The Copenhagen service was withdrawn in December 1981.

By 1980 the oil boom was boosting traffic figures at Aberdeen, and in March of that year BAC One-Eleven jets were introduced onto the Aberdeen-Manchester route. The oil industry was also responsible for the first visit to Aberdeen of a Lockheed Tristar wide-bodied

British Airways ATP G-MAUD at Aberdeen in August 2004. *(Author)*

Saab 340 G-GNTI in an all-white colour scheme with small British Airways Express titles, at Aberdeen in 1997. *(Author)*

British Airways Saab 340 G-LGNF at Aberdeen in May 2003. *(Author)*

British Airways Twin Otter G-BVVK at the airport terminal on the beach at Barra in May 2005. *(Mrs June Scott)*

British Airways Saab 340 G-LGNH landing at Aberdeen in September 2005. *(Author)*

jet. The 350-seat British Airways machine was operating one of four flights organised by Total Oil to take its employees away on weekend trips. The Tristar flew empty into Aberdeen at around 1030hrs on 8 May 1981 and picked up 180 passengers before flying to Gatwick to take on more trippers and continuing onwards to Tangier.

In September 1981 British Airways published a Survival Plan which called for the closure of the Scottish internal network unless anticipated losses could be eliminated. Scottish staff were invited to join a working party aimed at finding ways of avoiding a projected loss of £4 million in 1982/3 and operating at a profit thereafter. To achieve this aim it was decided to replace the remaining seven Viscounts with five more HS748s. A target of around £1 million profit was set for 1982/3, with 275,000 passengers to be carried in 1983/4 and revenue of £11 million to be earned in that financial year.

On 29 March 1982 the first HS748 service on the Aberdeen-Inverness-Stornoway route took place, and on the same day the last British Airways Viscount service out of Aberdeen was operated to Glasgow. The days of the Viscount were now numbered, and on 27 March 1982 a special farewell trip from Glasgow to Kirkwall took place. Viscount 806s G-AOYL, G-AOYM, G-AOYO and G-APIM, commanded by Captains Jim MacDonald, Roger Sawyer, Peter Brown and Elliott Stenhouse, flew to Kirkwall to mark twenty-five years of Viscount service on the route. Around 280 passengers, including former and current crew members, took part in the trip, which included a Viscount Farewell Dinner Dance at the Albert Ballroom in Kirkwall at which airline-style boxed

British Regional Airlines began operating Embraer 145s on cross-border routes for British Airways in October 1997. This is G-EMBF at Aberdeen in July 2000. *(Author)*

meals were served. The next day the passengers toured the island by coach before flying back to Glasgow in the Viscounts, whose cabins were festooned with balloons. Each passenger paid £35 for the trip, and the pilots and cabin crew gave their services free as well as contributing their £35. The four aircraft departed Kirkwall at lunchtime and made a low flypast over the airport and the town, watched by hundreds of spectators, before setting course for Glasgow via another flypast over Wick. The trip was organised by Jack Ridgeway, who served with BEA and then British Airways as station manager at Kirkwall airport for nearly twenty-five years.

In April 1982 the British Airways Highlands Division was established as an autonomous unit in an attempt to reverse the losses on the Scottish internal routes. The division was given a two-year period in which to prove itself, during which it was to be protected from direct competition. The total staff of 600 was to be reduced to 184 by the adoption of new working practices. At a typical smaller airport there was to be a ground staff of just three. The HS748s were to be commanded by experienced senior first officers instead of captains. As well as flying the aircraft they were expected to do their own flight planning, supervise refuelling and carry out the checks done by ground staff at large airports such as Glasgow and Edinburgh. The co-pilots were required to help with the loading of cargo and mail, and the cabin crew were to check in passengers and escort them to and from the aircraft at en route stops. In the event, a loss of £259,000 was incurred during 1982/3, but by 1983/4 this had been converted into a small profit. On 8 May 1982 the last Viscounts were retired. The last service was operated by series 806 G-AOYM on the Sumburgh-Kirkwall-Inverness-Glasgow route under the call sign *Speedbird 5721*.

The Aberdeen-Inverness route was dropped at the end of March 1983, after just one year of operation. It had averaged only ten passengers on each forty-four-seat HS748 service. However, on 27 March a second daily rotation was introduced on the Glasgow-Inverness route, and the twice-daily Aberdeen-Manchester-Paris connection was replaced by a same-aircraft through flight via Glasgow, operating five times weekly. In June 1983 Jetstream 31 aircraft leased from Birmingham Executive Airways were introduced onto Aberdeen-Birmingham services, and an Edinburgh-Jersey service commenced.

The successful introduction of the HS748s led to an order for a further three series 2A/Bs, one fitted with a freight door. These were to replace three examples being leased from Dan-Air, and the first machine was delivered to Glasgow on 13 December 1984. By 1989 the Highlands Division would be operating twelve HS748s, based at Glasgow and Aberdeen, and at various times over the years British Airways would operate a total of seventeen including leased examples. One of the original pair was involved in an incident at Sumburgh in November 1983. G-BCOF was landing in sleet and crosswinds after a service from Aberdeen and Kirkwall, when Captain Mike Young experienced poor braking response after touchdown and, as a precaution, decided to take the aircraft off the side of the runway and onto the grass. The seventeen passengers were unhurt.

On 26 March 1984 the Aberdeen-Edinburgh service, which had been dropped on the formation of the Highlands Division, was reinstated, and on 1 April the division won its first oil industry contract. This was for the provision of seats between Aberdeen and Glasgow for Britoil. Ten seats were to be blocked off on each scheduled service, equating to about 12,000 seats on each of the two years covered by the contract. Air Ecosse had previously been supplying seats to Britoil on a charter basis, and the deal was worth around £300,000 to British Airways.

A special HS748 flight to Kirkwall was operated from Aberdeen on 6 May 1984 to commemorate the fiftieth anniversary of Captain Fresson's first service over the route. Kirkwall airport, which was normally closed on Sundays, was opened specially for the flight, whose forty-eight passengers had each paid £25 for the trip which included a buffet lunch and a sightseeing coach tour.

During the spring of 1985 the services from Aberdeen to Birmingham and Manchester were being operated by Jetstream 31s of Birmingham Executive Airways and Peregrine Air Services respectively, but from 1 June these aircraft were supplanted by British Airways HS748s. For the summer of 1985 the 748s were also used on the Highlands Division's first scheduled international route, a seasonal service from Kirkwall to Bergen via Sumburgh,

British Airways HS748 G-BCOF at Inverness on 13 August 1982. *(L.F. Sarjeant)*

Saab 340 G-BNTE in the British Airways 'Mountain of the Birds' tail livery. *(Kieran Murray)*

British Airways Saab 340 G-LGNG in June 2006. *(Kieran Murray)*

and on 18 November the type was used to inaugurate Aberdeen-Birmingham-Southampton scheduled services.

The HS748's replacement was to be the British Aerospace ATP (Advanced Turbo-Prop), eight of which were ordered in 1988. Deliveries began on 22 December 1988, and all eight had entered service by July 1989. The sixty-four-seat ATP first entered service in January 1989, operating from Aberdeen, Edinburgh and Glasgow to Birmingham and Manchester, and also on the Internal German Services network. Another five were ordered in August 1991 and another example, which was being operated on lease from British Aerospace, was purchased in July 1994 to take the total to fourteen. After the type was withdrawn from the Internal German Services network the examples used were returned to the UK for use by the Highlands Division.

The last HS748 service out of Glasgow took place on 27 March 1992, and the final British Airways HS748 service was operated on 15 April of that year.

In March 1992 the formation of British Airways Regional was announced. It was a new subsidiary set up to run and improve profitability on services out of Birmingham and Manchester and within Scotland. As well as operating domestic services British Airways Regional also operated direct flights to New York from regional airports. A two-class service between Glasgow and New York was introduced for the summer of 1993, and ran each summer until 1999.

HS748 G-ATMJ in 'British' livery at Inverness on 5 March 1983. *(L.F. Sarjeant)*

HS748 G-ATMJ in 'British' livery at Inverness on 5 March 1983. *(L.F. Sarjeant)*

British Airways Express Shorts 360 G-BWMZ wears small Loganair stickers at Wick in 1995. *(Author)*

On 21 September 1992 ATP G-BTPM was involved in an emergency at Sumburgh. The aircraft was inbound on a scheduled service from Aberdeen with forty-three passengers and four crew aboard, when traces of smoke and a burning smell were detected in the passenger cabin as it passed through 9,000ft on approach to Sumburgh. As the aircraft decelerated after touchdown smoke was observed coming from the starboard engine. An emergency evacuation was carried out with no injuries and no damage to the aircraft. The source of the smoke was later traced to an oil leakage caused by the fracture of the number five bearing cage. The Air Accident Investigation Board report noted that this was the eighth occasion this had happened to members of the ATP fleet.

In 1993 British Airways entered into the first of many franchising agreements involving its Scottish routes. In that year a five-year agreement was signed with CityFlyer Express, for flights under the British Airways Express brand. In May of that year an agreement was also reached on the purchase of Brymon Airways by British Airways, and Brymon aircraft began appearing in British Airways colours from August 1993. In April 1994 British Airways and Loganair announced plans to protect British Airways' loss-making Scottish routes, with Loganair entering into a franchise arrangement to operate services on several of the routes in British Airways Express livery from July 1994. In January 1995 Manx Airlines (Europe) also became a franchisee, operating ATPs and Jetstream 41s in British Airways Express colours.

British Airways ATP G-BTPM at Sumburgh on 21 September 1992 with emergency evacuation chutes deployed after its landing incident. *(Kieran Murray)*

On 1 September 1996 the Airlines of Britain Group took over six loss-making routes serving Kirkwall, Lerwick and the Western Isles. Manx Airlines (Europe) was grouped together with Loganair to form British Regional Airlines and began operating on the Glasgow-Benbecula and Stornoway-Inverness routes with ATP aircraft, and a Saab 340 was leased from Business Air to serve the route from Aberdeen to Kirkwall and Sumburgh. Yet on 28 February 1997 a management buy-out saw Loganair leave the combine and operate independently once more. Britain's first Embraer 145 jets were introduced by British Regional Airlines on cross-border routes to England in October 1997. A further development took place in 1998 when the routes from Aberdeen to Manchester and Birmingham were transferred to British Airways subsidiary Brymon Airways, and Brymon ordered eight new Dash Eight turbo-props for its franchise operations. By now the days of the ATP on British Airways routes were numbered, and the final service operated from Edinburgh to Manchester as flight BA1865 on 26 January 1999.

On 9 February 1998 British Regional Airlines Shorts 360 G-BLGB was operating a British Airways service from Benbecula to Stornoway with twenty-six passengers and four crew aboard. A heavy landing was made at Stornoway, the left side of the aircraft went down and the aircraft slewed to the left. There were no serious injuries to the occupants but the aircraft was considered a write-off.

A British Airways Express DHC-8 landing at Aberdeen in 1996. *(Author)*

Shorts 360 G-BWMZ in British Airways Express livery at Wick in 1995. *(Kieran Murray)*

British Midland Commuter Saab 340 G-GNTI at Aberdeen in 1997. *(Author)*

Business Air Shorts 360 G-OJSY. (Kieran Murray)

Business Air Saab 340 G–BGNA and supporting air and ground crew at Sumburgh on 1 November 1996, after the airline's inaugural scheduled service from Aberdeen. *(Kieran Murray)*

Loganair Saab 340 G-LGNA wears the British Airways tartan tail livery at Inverness on 14 August 2000. *(L.F. Sarjeant)*

In 1998 the CityFlyer Express franchise agreement came to an end, and British Airways announced its intention of acquiring the airline as a subsidiary with effect from November 1999. In 2000 British Regional Airlines was operating franchise services for British Airways on routes linking Aberdeen with Glasgow, Kirkwall, Sumburgh, Belfast, Cardiff, Leeds/Bradford and Southampton. The varied fleet included the ATP, Jetstream 41 and Shorts 360 turbo-props and BAe 146 and Embraer 145 regional jets. Services were also operated from Edinburgh to Belfast, Cardiff, Paris and Southampton, and from Glasgow to Belfast, Benbecula, Cardiff, Southampton and Stornoway, but the Stornoway-Inverness route passed to Loganair that year. In March 2001 the airline was bought by British Airways for £78 million. The Aberdeen-Kirkwall and Aberdeen-Sumburgh franchises were taken over by Loganair on 15 September 2001 when the lease on the Saab 340 expired.

In October 2001 British Airways combined its subsidiaries BA Regional and CitiExpress to create the second largest regional airline in Europe. On 28 March 2002 Brymon Airways and British Regional Airlines, which was now also a British Airways subsidiary, were merged, the combined company being re-branded as British Airways CitiExpress. It was renamed again on 1 February, this time as British Airways Connect, but on 25 March 2007 the subsidiary was sold to Flybe, reputedly for a nominal £1, in a bid to stem losses of £1 million per week.

British Airways HS748 G-BOHY at Aberdeen in August 1989. *(Author)*

British Airways Express Jetstream 41 G-MAJH. *(Author)*

Loganair Jetstream 41 G-MAJH in British Airways Express livery at Inverness on 1 August 1998.
(*L.F. Sarjeant*)

British Airways Islander G–BJOP landing at Tingwall in 1999. *(Kieran Murray)*

British Airways ATP G-MANJ landing at Aberdeen. *(Author)*

British Airways also outsourced its entire Scottish passenger handling operations to handling agent Aviance, cutting 430 jobs from its payroll. By now, with the exception of the trunk routes to London, British Airways had no Scottish routes operated by its own aircraft.

CHAPTER FIVE

OTHER OPERATORS

SCOTTISH AIRLINES

Scottish Airlines was founded at Prestwick Airport on 1 January 1946 as the airline division of Scottish Aviation, notable for its overhaul and civil conversion work on many types such as the C-47 Dakota. It is not surprising, then, that its initial operations utilised Dakotas, a type that was to serve the airline throughout its history. On 16 January 1946 Dakota G-AGWS visited Dyce, Aberdeen, and took a party of VIPs, including members of the Aberdeen Chamber of Commerce, and the press on a local sightseeing flight. On 28 January the same aircraft inaugurated a scheduled service under contract to BEA from Prestwick to Belfast (Sydenham). The aircraft was configured to seat twenty-one passengers and the one-way fare was £1 10d. From 1 August 1946 until the end of July 1947 Dakota services from Prestwick to London (both direct and via Renfrew), from Renfrew to Belfast, and from Aberdeen to London via Edinburgh were operated under contract to BEA. Scottish Airlines also owned a Fokker F.22 which was chartered to BEA from 1 February–31 July 1947 for Glasgow-Belfast services. At the end of this period it was re-engined with Pratt and Whitney Twin Wasp engines and used for joy-riding from Prestwick. Dakota services were also operated for KLM on the Prestwick to Amsterdam route from July 1946 until 31 March 1947, and for Air France from Prestwick to Paris via Manchester.

Scottish Airlines had a financial interest in the Belgian airline COBETA, which opened a twice-weekly Brussels-Prestwick-Manchester service in July 1947. Start-up assistance, including the provision of Dakotas, was given to Luxembourg Airlines, and a 40 per cent stake was taken in Hellenic Airlines. From March 1948 Scottish Airlines operated a twice-

Scottish Airlines Avro York G-AMUM. *(L.F. Sarjeant)*

weekly London-Paris-Rome-Athens-Cairo service for this Greek airline, using converted Consolidated Liberator bombers. Scottish Air Express, a division of Scottish Airlines, was set up to market inclusive tour flights from Prestwick to European destinations; these flights included a series of fortnightly Dakota flights from Prestwick to Lisbon, where the passengers boarded an Anchor Line liner for a two-week cruise.

The airline's founder, David McIntyre, also had ambitious plans for a global network of scheduled services, including UK domestic routes, and flights from Prestwick to Europe, the Middle East and Far East, and the USA. Among them was a proposed Prestwick-New York scheduled service at a fare of £80 each way, and on 16 March 1946 Liberator II G-AGZH/AL571 was loaded with cargo and despatched from Prestwick on a survey flight to San Diego, California. Liberators were also operated under contract to Iceland Airways (Flugfelag Islands), flying Reykjavik-Prestwick-Copenhagen from 27 May 1946 until 10 April 1948, and Reykjavik-Gander-New York from 16 September 1946.

In June 1947 the fleet included five Liberators, thirteen Dakotas and the solitary Fokker F.22, which was withdrawn in August. Joy-riding was carried out using Airspeed Oxford G-AHDZ, joined later by Percival Proctors G-AHMP and G-AHNT. Supermarine Walrus amphibian G-AJNO was refurbished by Scottish Aviation for a proposed Scottish Airlines service to Brodick on the Isle of Arran, but this never came to fruition.

On 15 August 1947 two self-governing dominions, India and Pakistan, were created out of what had been the British colony of India. This led to racial violence between

Hindu and Muslim groups, and there was the urgent need to evacuate refugees from the fighting. An airlift was arranged, with BOAC acting as co-ordinating agent for the various independent operators involved. Scottish Airlines positioned five Dakotas out to Karachi as its contribution, and between them the airlines carried 8,500 refugees from India to Pakistan. Before the end of the year another airlift in the opposite direction was called for and this time Scottish Airlines sent six Dakotas. During October and November a further 41,000 refugees were carried to safety.

For the 1948 summer season two new holiday routes, from Prestwick to the Isle of Man and from Northolt to Zurich, were operated with Dakotas under BEA Associate Agreements. These allowed the independent airlines to operate limited scheduled services on routes that did not affect the national carrier's own commercial interests.

In 1948 Scottish Airlines joined another airlift, this time Operation Plainfare, the Berlin Airlift. One Liberator and two Dakotas were committed, and 116 freighter sorties and 381 fuel tanker sorties were flown into Berlin before the aircraft were temporarily withdrawn on 14 and 27 August respectively in order to take part in another airlift closer to home. A shortage of milk in mainland Britain had led to aircraft being chartered to fly milk in churns from Belfast to Blackpool and Liverpool. Scottish Airlines employed two Dakotas and two Liberators on this work from 31 August 1948 until mid-October. One Liberator was lost at Liverpool, but on 19 February the airline rejoined the Berlin Airlift, this time using two Liberator tankers before finally withdrawing permanently on 12 July. The Liberators were also used for ad hoc charters, one notable operation leaving Prestwick for Jamaica on 3 December 1948.

On 3 April 1949 Scottish Airlines crews took over the operation of BOAC's thrice-weekly Prestwick-Montreal Liberator freight service and maintained operations until 27 September During the period 1 June–3 September 1949 Dakota services from Prestwick to Manchester via Blackpool were operated under another BEA Associate Agreement, as was a Dragon Rapide service from Manchester to the Isle of Man via Blackpool. By November 1949 the fleet had dwindled to five Dakotas, four Liberators and a single Dragon Rapide. The last of the Liberators was finally withdrawn in October 1950.

On 9 June 1951 a Prestwick-Burtonwood (for Liverpool and Manchester)-Northolt scheduled Dakota service was inaugurated. In September of that year a restructuring of the organisation led to Scottish Airlines (Prestwick) being registered as an airline company and to its taking over the scheduled service and charter operations of Scottish Airlines. In the same month three Avro Yorks were purchased for use on Air Ministry contract for the carriage of military personnel to Montreal. For this purpose they were converted at Prestwick to accommodate fifty-two passengers in rear-facing seats. In 1951 the Prestwick-Isle of Man service was operated throughout the winter for the first time, with six-seat Dragon Rapides taking the place of Dakotas.

The February–March 1952 timetable of Bradshaw's *International Air Guide* showed Scottish Airlines (Prestwick) Dakota flight SA100 departing Prestwick at 0815hrs, calling at Burtonwood between 0930–0945hrs and arriving Northolt at 1100hrs. The return flight, SA101, in the evening left Northolt at 1815hrs, called at Burtonwood from 1930–1945hrs and arrived at Prestwick at 2100hrs. The free baggage allowance was 35lb. There was also a Prestwick-Isle of Man round trip on Mondays, Thursdays and Saturdays, operated as flights SA1 and SA2 by the Dragon Rapide. The Dakotas were also used for ad hoc charter flights, one such service carrying thirty-two staff of the retail furniture store A. Cochran and Sons, Newmilns Ltd, from Prestwick to Belfast in August 1952.

The Prestwick-Burtonwood-Northolt service came to an end in mid-February 1953, but by then the airline had started fulfilling another Air Ministry contract with the York fleet. This was for the transport of military cadets from Stansted to Montreal for twelve months from 30 January 1953. A base was set up at Stansted and further work for the Yorks came along in the form of cargo charters for Trans-Canada Air Lines between 7 March and 30 July 1953. During 1954 four more Yorks were acquired for yet more contracts, this time for troop flights to Malta, Cyprus and the Middle East. By the time these contracts terminated in 1958 five of the Yorks had been lost in accidents. The remaining two examples were then sold, reducing the fleet to just one Dakota, G-AMPP.

The final Isle of Man-Prestwick service was operated by G-AMPP on 25 September 1960. The aircraft was then utilised on ad hoc charters until 21 November, when it went into storage for the winter. Early in 1961 Scottish Airlines (Prestwick), its Prestwick-Isle of Man route licence, and Dakota G-AMPP were sold to Dan-Air.

Scottish Airlines' long-serving Dakota G-AMPP. *(Air-Britain)*

SCOT AIRWAYS

The airline known today as Scot Airways was established in November 1984 as Suckling Airways, named after its founders Roy and Merlyn Suckling. Air taxi and charter operations commenced from its Ipswich Airport base in 1986, and on 26 April of that year a scheduled service was inaugurated from Ipswich to Amsterdam via Manchester using a single Dornier 228 aircraft. By January 1988 the airline was also operating between Edinburgh and Norwich, with two round trips each weekday and one on Sundays.

In 1999 Brian Souter, chairman of the Perth-based Stagecoach Group, and his sister, Ann Gloag, purchased a 90 per cent stake in the airline for £5 million. On 13 October 1999 the company name was changed to Suckling Airways (Cambridge) Ltd, trading as Scot Airways, and the Dornier 328 turbo-props which had replaced the earlier Dornier 228 were repainted in a new livery which featured red tartan tailfins. Services from Dundee and Glasgow to London City Airport and from Cambridge to Edinburgh were operated, and in 2000 a Dundee-Manchester route was introduced.

For the winter of 2000–2001 Aberdeen was linked to London City under a code-sharing agreement with British European Airways, and other routes linked Amsterdam with Southampton and Cambridge, Guernsey with Southampton, and Edinburgh with London City. On 10 September 2001 an Inverness-London City service was inaugurated. However, in the aftermath of the terrorist attack on the World Trade Center on 11 September 2001,

Scot Airways Dornier Do328 G-BYMK at Inverness on 13 September 2001. *(L.F. Sarjeant)*

and the subsequent slump in air travel, the services out of Aberdeen, Glasgow, Norwich and Cambridge were axed and Dundee effectively became the operating base, although London City flights still operated from Edinburgh.

On 6 March 2002 the sixteen passengers and four crew of Dornier 328 G-BWIR had a lucky escape on take-off from Edinburgh on a service to London City. During the take-off roll the first officer saw a red 'Doors' warning light illuminate. He managed to bring the aircraft to a halt on the runway and taxied back to the terminal. During the rapid acceleration on take-off the cabin attendant had involuntarily grasped the door handle and the door had become unfastened, although it did not detach in the slipstream. Had it done so, being at the front of the cabin, it would have probably struck the engine on that side.

During 2004 the passenger loads had so recovered that ten Edinburgh-London City round trips were operated each day and the Dundee-London City route's frequency was increased

Scot Airways Do328 G-BYMK taxiing at Inverness on 21 September 2001. *(L.F. Sarjeant)*

to four times daily. On 9 May 2005, to combat competition from the BAe RJ jets of British Airways CityExpress on the Edinburgh-London City route, Scot Airways introduced its own jet equipment on the route. An eighty-seat BAe 146 leased from Titan Airways was used on one peak-hour round trip each weekday under a code-sharing agreement with Flybe, while Dornier 328s operated the rest of the services. During 2005 Scot Airways carried 180,000 passengers and generated a turnover of £22.7 million. By August 2006 the fleet stood at seven Dornier 328s.

On 18 September 2006 it was announced that Brian Souter and Ann Gloag had sold their entire shareholding back to Roy and Merlyn Suckling and Brian Souter had stood down as chairman. From 26 March 2007 the routes from Edinburgh and Dundee to London City came under a new code-sharing agreement with Cityjet for Air France, and under the same arrangement a new route from Belfast City Airport to London City was launched.

ACE SCOTLAND

ACE Scotland was a subsidiary of Aviation Charter Enterprises, and was formed to operate inclusive-tour charter flights from Glasgow to the Mediterranean during the summer of 1966. The parent company had acquired a number of Lockheed Constellation aircraft for its cargo charter work and one of these, L-749A Constellation G-ASYF, was transferred to ACE Scotland and flown to Scottish Aviation at Prestwick in January 1966 for conversion to an eighty-two-seat passenger configuration. On completion of this work it arrived at Glasgow Airport on 14 June 1966 and entered service, but it proved to be notoriously unreliable, consistently suffering from engine failures and oil leaks. The crews also complained of poor handling and sluggish performance. There was a story at the time that the cabin door had once become detached while the aircraft was on the ground at Glasgow and had fallen onto the apron in full view of the passengers.

By 30 June 1966 G-ASYF had returned to Scottish Aviation at Prestwick for more work. It then departed Prestwick for Glasgow but returned immediately with control problems and made an emergency landing. On inspection, a large quantity of water was found in the bottom of the fuselage. This had created fluctuations in the aircraft's centre of gravity and had resulted in an uncommanded pitch-up after take-off. Holes were made with the aid of a small hand-drill and the water was drained onto the tarmac.

On 18 August 1966 the aircraft was on a flight from Athens to Prestwick when poor weather at Prestwick forced it to divert to Glasgow. Later that day it was again ferried to Scottish Aviation at Prestwick. It is uncertain if any more services were operated after that date, but on 14 September 1966 Aviation Charter Enterprises and ACE Scotland ceased all flying and went into liquidation.

AIR SCOTLAND

Air Scotland was founded in November 2002 by Iraqi-born Dhia Al-Ali. At its official launch in January 2003 it was described as 'Scotland's first low-budget airline'. Mr Al-Ali said he was going to invest £47 million in the airline as part of a plan to make Scotland a transport hub for travel to Spain, Belgium and Scandinavia. He was reported to be seeking talks with Ryanair, easyJet, the Scottish Executive and Visit Scotland with a view to persuading passengers from Belgium and Scandinavia to fly to Spanish destinations via Scotland in order to take advantage of his cheaper fares. The initial routes were to be from Glasgow to Barcelona, Palma and Tenerife, and from Edinburgh to Barcelona, Palma, Alicante, Malaga and Fuerteventura. There would also be services from Aberdeen, initially to Barcelona. Two classes of travel would be offered: 'Thistle' (premium) class and 'Tartan' (economy) class. It was thought that the airline would create about 850 Scottish jobs, directly and indirectly, over the coming five years.

Operations began on 29 March 2003 to Spanish resorts, using two Boeing 757-200s of Electra Airlines. Air Scotland acted as ticket provider to Electra Airlines until 25 April 2003, when the Electra aircraft were grounded due to a dispute with the British Airports Authority over monies owed. The arrangement with Electra was terminated and Air Scotland then began using aircraft of Air Holland until the demise of that carrier, whereupon it switched to Greece Airways, which was also owned by Mr Al-Ani and which had been formed out of the assets of Electra Airlines. This time just one 233-seat Boeing 757, SX-BLW, was used.

In 2005 Air Scotland announced its intention of leasing two Lockheed Tristars for use on scheduled services between the UK and Iraq. A twice-weekly service from Glasgow to Baghdad via Stansted was proposed, and the wide-bodied jets were also intended for use on proposed flights from Glasgow to Miami, New York and Cuba, but none of these plans actually materialised.

At the beginning of 2005 Mr Al-Ani sold his stake in Air Scotland to the H.TOP Hotels Group of Barcelona. However, problems with the transfer of ownership led to bills going unpaid and the 757 being grounded at Palma, with passengers being stranded for up to 17 hours.

For the summer of 2006 services were scheduled from Glasgow to Alicante, Athens, Malaga, Girona and Palma, and from Manchester to Alicante, Barcelona, Girona, Malaga and Palma. The Boeing 757 was sold to jet2.com, and Airbus A320-211 SX-BLX was acquired to replace it. Plans to acquire a second-hand aircraft, to be based at Girona, and to change the airline name to topjetair were announced, but in December 2006 the Greek Civil Aviation Authority suspended Air Scotland's Air Operators Certificate. Operations ceased in February 2007.

FLYGLOBESPAN

Flyglobespan is the low-cost airline subsidiary of The Globespan Group plc, a company established in 1974. The airline operated its first service in April 2002, and initially used two Boeing 737-300s provided by Channel Express, on whose Air Operators Certificate they were operated. Services were initially operated from Edinburgh and Prestwick, although within months the Prestwick flights had been transferred to Glasgow Airport.

Flyglobespan acquired its own AOC in 2004, and made an operating profit of £3.7 million on turnover of £98 million during the year ending October 2004. By March 2005 the company was flying to fifteen destinations across Europe with nine aircraft. In May 2005 the airline launched its first UK domestic services, twice-daily flights from Glasgow and Edinburgh to Stansted in direct competition with easyJet. Standard fares from £19.99 each way and Flexible Business Fares from £59 each way were offered, and during 2005 the passenger figures increased by 50 per cent to almost 1.5 million.

The latest Boeing 737-800s were introduced in April 2005, Flyglobespan being the first UK airline to install winglets on them for faster climb performance and greater fuel efficiency. In 2005 the carrier was named Airline of The Year by BAA Scotland.

In February 2006 the domestic services were withdrawn following poor sales, and a projected Edinburgh-Bournemouth route was dropped. By the summer, however, Flyglobespan was operating out of Teesside, Liverpool, Stansted and Manchester in addition to Glasgow and Edinburgh, and had opened its first transatlantic service, from Glasgow to Sanford, Florida, using Boeing 767-300 wide-bodied aircraft in a three-class configuration. Plans were in hand to raise an extra £600 million to finance the purchase of ten more wide-bodied aircraft for new long-haul routes from Glasgow and Edinburgh to Canada, the USA and other destinations. In August 2006 the airline announced that it was to lease two new Boeing 787 Dreamliners from ILFC for ten years, with delivery scheduled for March and November 2010.

During the summer of 2007 Flyglobespan was flying long-haul services from Glasgow to Toronto, Orlando, Vancouver and Boston as well as summer sun services to Alicante, Athens, Barcelona, Cyprus, Faro, Gran Canaria, Ibiza, Lanzarote, Malaga, Palma and Tenerife. From Edinburgh the destinations of Alicante, Barcelona, Faro, Ibiza, Malaga, Murcia, Nice, Palma, Pula, Rome and Toronto were served, and there were also flights out of Aberdeen to Alicante, Barcelona, Cyprus, Faro, Murcia, Palma and Tenerife.

STRATHAIR

Strathallan Air Services, trading as Strathair, was formed in 1962 by Sir William Roberts as an air charter company based at Auchterarder airfield on his estate at Strathallan Castle in Perthshire. The first equipment consisted of Helio Courier short take-off and landing aircraft, and on 24 July 1964 one of these inaugurated an on-demand service to Portree on Skye to connect with BEA flights arriving at Glasgow and Edinburgh. The single-engined Helio Couriers were replaced by twin-engined Piper Aztecs, a Twin Commanche and a de Havilland Dove, and various charter flights were operated before Aztec G-ATLC opened a new scheduled service from Edinburgh to Dundee and Prestwick on 18 July 1966. From the beginning of August the route was taken over by Dove G-ASDD, the service acting mainly as a feeder connection for transatlantic flights at Prestwick, until it was abandoned on 2 September 1966 due to lack of support.

Earlier in the year Strathair had acquired its first Dakota aircraft. This was disposed of without seeing much use, but in April 1967 another example, G-AOGZ, was purchased and based at Edinburgh. This operated several flights out of Aberdeen, flew a charter from Edinburgh to Amsterdam on 19 May, and carried newspapers to Scotland during a rail dispute in July.

By the winter of 1967 the Dakota had been relocated to Aberdeen and from there it flew oil-rig support flights to Sumburgh and Teesside on behalf of BEA. Over the next year this type of work continued to occupy the aircraft, but in March 1968 the Dakota was sold. Air taxi operations continued with two Aztecs and the Dove, but by early 1971 only one Aztec remained in service. This was lost in a fatal accident at Gleneagles golf course in June 1971 and all operations then ceased.

PEREGRINE AIR SERVICES

Peregrine Air Services was formed as an air taxi operator at Inverness Airport in the summer of 1969. On 15 November 1972 a new base was opened at Aberdeen and an Aztec was based there. In April 1974 another Aztec was based at Sumburgh, and by 1976 at least two Aztecs were stationed at Aberdeen for oil-related charters. On 24 February 1982 a new hangar at Aberdeen was opened by Sir Douglas Bader

Jetstream 31 turbo-props were acquired, and from 1993 these were operated on behalf of British Airways on off-peak Aberdeen-Manchester services. In April 1984 Peregrine announced that it had secured a contract from Conoco for Aberdeen-Sumburgh charter flights with Jetstream 31 aircraft. Another contract, from Phillips Petroleum, entailed three roundt rips between Aberdeen and Norwich each week with eleven-seat Cessna 404 Titan aircraft.

During 1985 Peregrine applied for licences for scheduled services from Aberdeen to Gothenburg and Stockholm. Jetstream 31s were to be used with a flight duration of just over 2 hours, but services never started. Following the collapse of Air Ecosse in 1986 the assets and some of the route licences of that airline were taken over by Peregrine. In July of that year two Grumman Gulfstream 1 turbo-props arrived at the Aberdeen base. These had been operated as executive transports in the USA, and were converted to twenty-four-

Peregrine Air Services Twin Commanche G-AVJJ at Inverness in mid-July 1977. *(L.F. Sarjeant)*

A Peregrine Airways Jetstream 31 in flight. *(Via the late John Begg)*

seat configuration. They then replaced the Jetstream 31s on the British Airways Aberdeen-Manchester services, becoming the first airline-operated Gulfstreams in the UK. A third example followed in February 1987.

From 7 March 1989 the company was renamed Aberdeen Airways.

ABERDEEN AIRWAYS

On 7 March 1989 Aberdeen Airways was formed out of Peregrine Air Services. During the summer of that year, Gulfstream 1 aircraft operated scheduled services from Aberdeen to East Midlands Airport via Edinburgh. There were two round trips every weekday, plus an additional Edinburgh-East Midlands rotation on Tuesdays, Wednesdays and Thursdays. The Gulfstreams also operated a daily Aberdeen-Manchester service, all these schedules using the former Air Ecosse SM flight prefix. As well as operating passenger services one aircraft, G-BMPA, was allocated to the Post Office EMS Datapost contract which the company had gained.

In early 1990 two leased HS748 aircraft joined the fleet. These were then used on the Aberdeen-Edinburgh-East Midlands route, with Aberdeen-Manchester services still being operated by the Gulfstream 1 fleet. Over twelve months the number of passengers carried

Aberdeen Airways HS748 G-BMPA in Datapost/EMS livery at Edinburgh in September 1989. *(Author)*

The hulk of former Aberdeen Airways Gulfstream 1 G-BNCE still wears North East Express titles at Aberdeen in 1995. *(Author)*

Aberdeen Airways HS748 G-AZSU at Aberdeen in July 1990, still with Dan-Air tail logo. *(Author)*

between Aberdeen and the East Midlands grew from 14,000 to 24,000. At that time the airline had its administrative headquarters in a building adjacent to the main terminal at Aberdeen. It employed around fifty staff, including twenty pilots and fourteen engineers. The fleet comprised two HS748s, four Gulfstream 1s and two Cessna Titans. The company operated the only CAA-approved fixed-wing maintenance facility at Aberdeen Airport, covering 27,000ft on the east side of the airport.

The winter of 1990–1 saw the Cessna Titans operating Aberdeen-Edinburgh twice each weekday, with HS748 aircraft flying between Edinburgh and the East Midlands and the Gulfstream 1s providing two Aberdeen-Manchester round trips each weekday. There was also a new link between the East Midlands and Wick in Caithness. Two services operated each weekday, one routeing via Edinburgh and the other via Aberdeen, with HS748 or Gulfstream equipment being used.

On 8 January 1991 Aberdeen Airways entered financial administration. The company was taken over by Air Provence on 11 February and the operating base was transferred to East Midlands Airport shortly afterwards. From May 1991 twice-daily services between Teesside and London (Gatwick) were operated under the name of North East Express, but operations were finally suspended in November 1992.

Aberdeen Airways Cessna Titan G-BKWA in the maintenance area at Aberdeen in April 1990, with a Gulfstream 1 in the background. *(Author)*

BON ACCORD AIRWAYS

In September 1992 John Begg, an experienced Aberdeen charter broker formerly with Peregrine Air Services and Aberdeen Airways, founded Bon Accord Airways, based at Aberdeen Airport. Within two months of its formation the carrier was invited to tender for a Post Office contract for the provision of mail flights between Aberdeen and Edinburgh on each weekday night. The contract was awarded at the end of October 1992 and Embraer Bandeirante G-OJAY was leased to carry out the flights, also operating passenger charters during the day in an eighteen-seat configuration. In January 1993 the lease on this aircraft expired and another Bandeirant, G-BGYV, was leased from Jersey European Airways in its place.

On 4 February 1993 G-BGYV was chartered by the Disaster Unit of the Overseas Development Administration to transport an underwater camera and its support equipment and two technicians from Aberdeen to Split in the former Yugoslavia. The aircraft made the outward journey in a total flying time of 7½ hours, routeing via Clermont Ferrand where a 40-minute refuelling stop was made. On 18 February the aircraft was named *City of Aberdeen* by the Lord Provost of the city, but it was soon to be replaced by a larger machine. At the end

Business Air Bandeirante G-BGYV undergoing maintenance at Aberdeen in August 1990. *(Author)*

of February a contract was awarded by Amarada Hess for the movement of oil rig personnel and freight between Aberdeen and Sumburgh and the Bandeirante was replaced by the thirty-seat Shorts 330 G-BITW leased from Celtic Airways (later to be replaced by G-BJLK). The flights operated on Wednesdays and Fridays under flight number BON 401.

More ad hoc charters were operated in March 1993, including an urgent flight for Aberdeen University, transporting several hundred kilos of documentation from Aberdeen to Shetland for a seminar, and a sub-charter for British Airways on 22 March when the aircraft for their scheduled evening service from Aberdeen to Glasgow and back was unserviceable. On 21 May Celtic Airways ceased trading and their Shorts 330 G-BJLK was repossessed, so Bon Accord Airways needed to find a replacement in a hurry. There was nothing suitable available at short notice in the UK, so special dispensation was granted by the CAA for the lease of Twin Otter LN-FAL from Coast Air as a temporary measure. A more permanent answer was found on 21 July 1993 when a lease agreement was signed for the former Aer Lingus Shorts 360 G-CLAS, which Bon Accord named *St Ninian*. Its first service was a company outing from Edinburgh to Islay to visit a distillery. The Royal Mail flights between Aberdeen and Edinburgh continued through the summer under the flight number BON 101, and during the year contract flying was also carried out between Aberdeen, Newcastle and Esbjerg for Ross Offshore.

Bon Accord Airways Shorts 360 G-CLAS at Sumburgh, still in its basic Aer Lingus colours. *(Kieran Murray)*

In September 1993 Amarada Hess signed up for a further 100 trips between Aberdeen and Shetland, but the Post Office contract was terminated by Bon Accord as they were still being paid the rates originally agreed when the Bandeirante was in use, and these rates were no longer profitable when applied to Shorts 360 operations. In December 1993 the former Soviet leader Mikhail Gorbachev and his wife visited Aberdeen where he received the Freedom of the City. Bon Accord Airways were contracted to provide air transportation, for which they sub-contracted a BAe 146 to operate charter flights from Leipzig to Aberdeen and return.

March 1994 saw the beginning of a short-term contract for Stena A/S of Norway for the transfer of oil rig personnel between Aberdeen, Edinburgh and Stavanger. In July 1994 crew change flights were operated to Swansea for the Marathon rig Sedco 711, and other ad hoc charters that year included the transportation of the owners of a Shetland fishing company and their wives from Shetland to Molde for the launch of a new trawler. In July and August of that year a new venture was inaugurated by Bon Accord, providing the air element of a series of week-long 'aerial cruises' around the Scottish Highlands and Islands for Island Holidays of Comrie.

In the spring of 1995 the airline was awarded a twelve-month contract for Thursday flights between Aberdeen and Cork for Marathon Oil. Prior to this Bon Accord had been chosen by Texaco for the provision of Aberdeen-Shetland flights three times each week for a year. The 'aerial cruise' flights the previous summer had been well received, especially by Americans touring Europe, and a further series for that summer was advertised as the Great Scottish Air Cruise 1995. There were departures on six Saturdays during July and August. Each trip, of seven days duration, included flights in Bon Accord's Shorts 360 and overnight stays in the best hotels. At the end of the summer, however, the airline experienced a slump in demand for its services and it ceased operations in November 1995.

BOAC

On 18 December 1972 the state-owned long-haul airline BOAC launched feeder services between Prestwick and Edinburgh to connect with its transatlantic services through Prestwick. To operate these flights, two Viscount 701 turbo-props were leased from Cambrian Airways and repainted in full BOAC livery. The two aircraft, G-AMOG and G-AMON, were refitted in a fifty-four-seat configuration and were named *Scottish Prince* and *Scottish Princess* respectively. The service was later extended to Aberdeen on a three-times-weekly basis and was claimed to offer the fastest connection between Aberdeen and Houston for the important oil market. Feeder services were also operated between Belfast and Prestwick. The contract for the feeder services was later transferred to British Midland Airways, which also used Viscounts.

ABERDEEN LONDON EXPRESS

Aberdeen London Express was established on 8 April 1993 and gained a licence to operate scheduled services between Aberdeen and London (Stansted). Services commenced on 31 October 1994, using a 104-seat BAC One-Eleven series 500 leased from European Aviation Air Charter and wearing their livery. The flights, which were in direct competition with Air UK on the same route, offered seats at £60 one-way. Flight EAF5000 operated from Aberdeen to Stansted at 0715hrs on Mondays-Fridays, and on Fridays only there was an additional service, EAF5004, at 2000hrs. In the opposite direction, flight EAF5003 left Stansted at 1900hrs on Mondays-Thursdays and at 1800hrs on Fridays, and there was a flight, EAF5005, at 1900hrs on Sundays.

Despite promises of support from the oil industry in the form of block bookings, the service was not a success and operations ceased on 6 December 1994.

LAKESIDE AVIATION

On 15 April 1991 Lakeside Aviation operated its first service, an oil-related charter flight from Aberdeen to Bergen at 0700hrs using a Cessna 404 Titan. On its arrival back at Aberdeen the aircraft uplifted six businessmen and flew them to Manchester.

Lakeside Aviation Cessna 404 G-LAKD at Aberdeen in May 1991. *(Author)*

The company had been formed in early 1991, and its fleet consisted of two former Aberdeen Airways Cessna 404s, G-LAKC and G-LAKD. During 1991 crew change flights were operated from Aberdeen to Shetland, Stavanger and Bergen, and other work included the repatriation of a seriously ill seaman from Glasgow to Quimper. A party of eight Americans were transported from Edinburgh to Chester for a day's sightseeing, and a group of oilmen were taken to Cork for a golfing weekend. The chairman of the CAA used the company's aircraft for a tour of Scottish airports, and a local sightseeing flight over Aberdeen Harbour was operated during the visit of the Tall Ships flotilla. Regular crew change flights were made from Aberdeen to Orkney, servicing the Elf Enterprise oil terminal at Flotta.

Early in 1992 an application was made for a scheduled service licence from Aberdeen to Barrow-in-Furness. This would have commenced in mid-January, with one rotation on each weekday using a Cessna 404 in an eleven-seat configuration, but it did not come to fruition. The company also acquired Jetstream 31 aircraft and proposed operating these on a scheduled service between Carlisle and Biggin Hill under the name of Lakeside North West. Attempts to obtain grants for this from the local authorities at Carlisle proved unsuccessful.

AIR ECOSSE

Air Ecosse was formed in June 1977 by Biggin Hill-based Fairflight Ltd. Its initial purpose was the operation of oil-related charters from Aberdeen and in that year it commenced flights from Aberdeen to Flotta on Orkney under a contract with Occidental Oil. In April 1978 the company opened a new hangar on the east side of Aberdeen Airport and on 6 June Air Ecosse and Bolt's Motor Garage Ltd formed an associate company called Air Shetland, based at Tingwall airfield on Shetland. In September 1978 Air Ecosse arranged for an Embraer Xingu demonstration aircraft to be brought to Aberdeen from that year's Farnborough Air Show for demonstration to local oil companies. The Xingu was in the livery of Air Shetland and was evaluated as a potential upmarket replacement for aircraft such as the Piper Navajo Chieftain currently operated by Air Ecosse.

On 30 July 1979 Air Ecosse commenced scheduled service operations with a Dundee-Aberdeen-Wick route. Three daily round trips were provided, with one of them continuing onwards to Shetland. The company was still seeking charter work as well, and on 1 April 1980 it began fulfilling a new contact from BNOC for Aberdeen-Glasgow flights. Three round trips were operated each day with Embraer Bandeirante turbo-props. In 1982 the scheduled service to Shetland was extended to Vagar in the Faroe Islands, although both the Vagar and Shetland extensions were to be discontinued by 1983. During 1982 Air Ecosse carried around 200,000 passengers on scheduled and charter flights.

1983 was a year of expansion. On 19 January the airline took delivery of its first Shorts 360 and converted an option on a second example into a firm order. The Shorts 360 was used to launch Datapost flights from Aberdeen to Edinburgh and Luton in January and a new

Bandeirante G-BSVT of Air Ecosse subsidiary Air Shetland at Biggin Hill on 1 November 1980. (L.F. Sarjeant)

scheduled service from Dundee to Heathrow via Carlisle on 4 August. Scheduled services were also inaugurated from Carlisle to the Isle of Man during the year, and the fleet for 1983 had grown to include seven eighteen-seat Bandeirantes and two Shorts 360s. On 20 April 1983, however, Twin Otter G-STUD, operated by Air Ecosse on charter to Occidental Oil, was involved in an accident at Flotta. The aircraft was on a charter from Aberdeen, with ten passengers and two crew aboard, and was attempting to land in a strong crosswind when the left wing began to rise and the pilot could not prevent it rising further. The right wing came into contact with the ground and the aircraft went through the airfield boundary fence and came to rest on its left side with both wings detached. Two of the people aboard were slightly hurt.

For the summer of 1983 the Air Ecosse timetable included services linking Aberdeen with Belfast, Dublin, Glasgow, Prestwick, Liverpool, Manchester and Wick. The services to Prestwick were timed to connect with Air Canada and Northwest Airlines transatlantic flights, and on Saturdays a coach connection to Dundee linked up with Dundee-Isle of Man services. From Dundee it was also possible to fly to Heathrow via Carlisle and to Manchester, and services also operated from Belfast to Glasgow and Prestwick. Following the collapse of Inter-City Airlines in 1983 Air Ecosse operated the Aberdeen-Edinburgh-East Midlands route on a temporary basis for some six weeks with a Shorts 330, and

Air Ecosse Trislander G-BDER at Biggin Hill on 1 November 1980. *(L.F. Sarjeant)*

was granted a full licence for the route in September. The airline had also expressed a desire to start up direct Aberdeen-Paris and Aberdeen-Hamburg services, stating that aircraft such as the thirty-seat Embraer Brasilia turbo-prop would be used if the licences were granted.

In 1983 Air Ecosse applied for its most ambitious route licence yet, for services from Aberdeen to Heathrow in direct competition with British Airways. The application requested three round trips each day, initially using BAC One-Eleven jets, although the stated intention was to acquire brand new aircraft such as the BAe 146 if the licence was granted. A normal one-way fare of 30 per cent less than British Airways' £69 fare was proposed, and in anticipation of the licence being granted Air Ecosse leased BAC One-Eleven G-AXMU in a ninety-seat layout from British Island Airways for the period 23 January–6 February 1984. The aircraft was named *Bon Accord* in a ceremony at Aberdeen Airport, at which Air Ecosse director Colin Pollard stated that direct services from Aberdeen to continental Europe and even North Africa would be opened once a sound revenue base had been secured from the proposed Heathrow route. British Midland, Air UK and Dan-Air had also applied for the Heathrow route, but in the end it was granted to none of the applicants and British Airways kept its monopoly for the immediate future.

In March 1984 it was announced that British Airways Highlands Division had been awarded the Britoil Aberdeen-Glasgow contract at the expense of Air Ecosse, and on 20 July of that year Air Ecosse said that it would be making twenty of its 160 staff redundant, the majority of the

Air Ecosse Shorts 360 in Datapost livery at Aberdeen on 21 May 1983. (L.F. Sarjeant)

redundancies being at the Aberdeen base. During the winter of 1984–5 the Glasgow-Belfast, Glasgow-Dublin and Aberdeen-Liverpool routes were closed down and the airline disposed of its two remaining Bandeirantes. Further financial losses were incurred in 1985 and Air Ecosse suspended operations out of Carlisle, transferring the daily Heathrow flights to Euroair.

On 29 November 1985 Air Ecosse was taken over by Crown International Airways. Plans for an expanded flight programme for the summer of 1986 were announced, and a new aircraft livery and hostess uniform were unveiled, but Air Ecosse ceased operations in 1986.

CITYSTAR AIRLINES

Although affiliated to the Icelandic domestic airline Landsflug EHF, CityStar Airlines was an Aberdeen-registered company, with shareholders in both Iceland and the UK. The airline inaugurated scheduled services on 28 March 2005 with weekday flights between Aberdeen and Oslo. The initial equipment was a single Dornier Do328 turbo-prop, but during that month CityStar acquired a controlling interest in Landsflug and ordered a second example. In scheduled service the Dorniers were normally fitted with thirty-two leather club-style seats. The cabin crew wore a deep red uniform that was designed by the airline's cabin crew director, Lesley-Anne Cairns, and the cabin crew trainer, Nicki Wharburton. The aircraft were also

1. The hulk of former Aberdeen Airways Gulfstream 1 G-BNCE still carries North East Express stickers at Aberdeen in 1995. *(Author)*

2. British Airways Express DHC-7 G-BRYA landing at Aberdeen in April 1996. *(Author)*

3. Air Ecosse Bandeirante G-MOBL at Manchester for a service to Dundee in 1980. *(Author)*

4. Alidair Scotland Viscount 735 G-BFMW at Manchester in 1980. *(Author)*

5. Highland Airways Shorts 360 G-BNDM at Aberdeen in 1997. (*Author*)

6. Brymon Airways DHC-7 G-BRYA in special 'Puffin' livery, landing at Aberdeen in 1997. (*Author*)

Above: 7. A Highland Express timetable from May–October 1987. *(Author's collection)*

Right: 8. An Aberdeen Airways timetable from March–October 1989. *(Author's collection)*

9. Bond Air Services King Air 200 G-SBAS at their base at Aberdeen in 1995. *(Author)*

10. Loch Lomond Seaplanes Cessna 206 G-OLLS in the static park at the 2004 RAF Leuchars air show. *(Author)*

11. British Airways Viscount 802 G-AOHW at Glasgow in 1975. *(Author)*

12. British World Viscount G-PFBT at Edinburgh in Parcelforce livery in 1994. *(Author)*

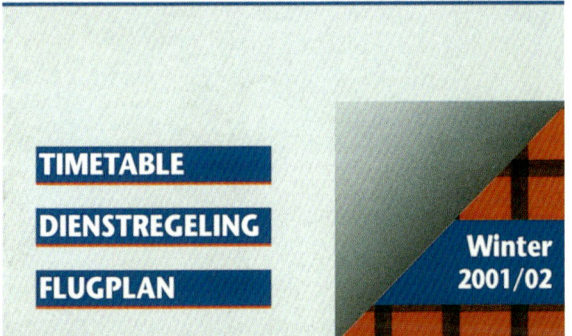

13. A Scot Airways timetable from 2001–2. Most of the flights used their own fleet of Fairchild aircraft, the Dornier 328-100. *(Author's collection)*

14. British Midland Commuter Embraer 145 G-RJXC taxiing at Aberdeen. *(Author)*

15. Scottish Air Ambulance Eurocopter EC-135 G-SASA at the RAF Lossiemouth open day in May 2001. *(Author)*

16. Air UK took over the east coast route network of Air Anglia on amalgamation, and continued to use Fokker F-27s on services from Aberdeen and Edinburgh. *(Author)*

17. Loganair Jetstream 31 G-LOGT on display at the Prestwick Air Show. *(Author)*

18. BEA Scottish Viscount 802 G-AOHI, a long way from home at Gatwick Airport in 1972. *(Author)*

19. Flightline Bandeirante G-FLTY at Aberdeen on the Parcelforce contract. *(Author)*

20. Tingwall, 2005. *(Kieran Murray)*

21. A British World Airways ATP leaves Scatsta for Aberdeen in October 2000. The oil installation is visible in the background. *(Kieran Murray)*

22. A collection of British Airways Express aircraft in May 1996. Islander G–BEDZ, Shorts 360s G–ISLE and G–LEGS, and ATP G–BTPA. *(Kieran Murray)*

23. Three Flightline BAe 146s pictured in 2005. *(Kieran Murray)*

24. Captain Eric Starling (left) and First Officer Davie Fielding in the cockpit of a British Airways ATP on 3 June 1996, to commemorate the sixtieth anniversary of Captain Starling's operation of the first service on the route in a de Havilland Rapide. *(Kieran Murray)*

25. British Airways Saab 340 G-LGNB at Kirkwall. *(Kieran Murray)*

26. The captain and ground crew of a BEA Herald at Glasgow in 1972–3. The group includes Donald Craig (third from right, back row) and George Gray (first on right, back row). *(Doreen Currie)*

27. British Airways' last ATP service from Sumburgh to Aberdeen departs in July 2005. The type was replaced by Saab 340s. *(Kieran Murray)*

28. British Airways ATP G-BTPM departs Sumburgh in April 1992 on the first ATP schedule to Aberdeen. *(Kieran Murray)*

29. Sumburgh, August 2006. *(Kieran Murray)*

30. Unst, 1995. *(Kieran Murray)*

31. Scatsta, July 2006, with BAe 146 departing. *(Kieran Murray)*

available for charter, and had the range to reach places such as Porto, Zagreb and Warsaw from Aberdeen with a full load of passengers. During the first three months of operations charters were in fact operated to Reykjavik, Trondheim, Manchester, Cardiff and Luxembourg.

On 11 July 2005 CityStar commenced an Aberdeen-Blackpool scheduled service. This was part-funded by the Scottish Executive's Route Development Fund and operated once daily on weekdays, but was not a commercial success and was suspended on 23 December 2005. A more successful new route was the Aberdeen-Stavanger-Kristiansund service which was inaugurated on 10 October 2005 with two round trips each weekday. Three Dornier 328 turbo-props were in service by then, and in March 2006 CityStar took delivery of its first Dornier 328Jet, in an executive configuration for use on charters out of both Aberdeen and Reykjavik. By that time the airline had grown from its initial single aircraft and twelve staff to encompass six Dorniers, ninety-six personnel and its own maintenance organisation.

A setback occurred on 22 June 2006 when Dornier 328 TF-CSB overran the runway at Aberdeen, at the end of scheduled service flight X9308 from Stavanger. Fortunately, no one was injured in the incident, and after investigations the aircraft was returned to service four days later and CityStar resumed normal operations.

More route development took place in 2007. On 29 May a new Aberdeen-Bergen service was launched with one round trip each weekday, and on 6 August an extension to Alesund was added to connect with the twice-daily flights between Aberdeen and Stavanger.

On 25 November 2007 CityStar Dornier 328 TF-CSB was involved in a collision with some mobile steps at Aberdeen airport, which resulted in the aircraft being taken out of service. Substitute aircraft had to be chartered from other couriers, and the knock-on effect of this led to the termination of CityStar operations at midnight on 30 January 2008.

CityStar Airlines Dornier 328 TF-CSA at Aberdeen in September 2005. (Author)

BRYMON AIRWAYS

Brymon Airways was founded on 26 January 1970, and for many years specialised in the operation of scheduled services around the West Country with Twin Otter aircraft based at Plymouth. However, the airline began a long-standing involvement with the North Sea oil industry on 25 September 1981 when it was awarded a contract for charter flights between Aberdeen and Unst on behalf of Chevron Petroleum. Two Dash Seven aircraft were purchased to fulfil this contract, and when they were not busy on this work they were available for ad hoc charter flights. Early in 1983 one of them was hired by the Mackey Brothers travel agency to carry the Dundee United football team to Stavanger for a UEFA Cup match.

On 2 April 1983 a scheduled service from Aberdeen to Newquay and Plymouth was inaugurated, operating on Saturdays with Dash Seven aircraft in a fifty-seat configuration. The return fare to Plymouth was £91. In March 1984 Brymon proposed using the Dash Sevens on a scheduled service between Aberdeen and the proposed London STOLPORT (later to become a reality as London City Airport), subject to government approval. The company was also interested in operating between Aberdeen and Sheffield, where there were also plans for a STOLPORT. These plans did not come to fruition but steady progress was maintained on the existing routes, and on 18 August Brymon carried its 100,000th passenger on the oil charter service to Unst.

By the winter of 1987–8 the routeing of the scheduled service to the West Country had been amended, with flights from Aberdeen calling at Plymouth first, then continuing onwards to Newquay before returning direct to Aberdeen. A special return fare of £136 between Aberdeen and Plymouth or Newquay was on offer, and by the summer of 1991 Brymon was also operating to Bristol. The weekday services from Aberdeen routed via Newcastle and there were also direct flights from Edinburgh and Glasgow. All the flights to Bristol were operated by Dash Eight turbo-props.

Brymon Airways DHC-7 G-BRYD in the static park at the RAF Leuchars Air Show in September 1991. (*Author*)

In October 1992 Brymon Airways was merged with British European Airways to form Brymon European Airways. However, the following year the two airlines were de-merged, with Maersk Air acquiring British European Airways and Brymon Airways becoming a wholly-owned British Airways subsidiary in August 1993. The Brymon aircraft were painted in British Airways Express livery. For the summer of 1993 two Aberdeen-Unst round trips were operated each weekday on the oil contract with Dash Sevens in a forty-six-seat layout. The Dash Eights were used on a weekday Aberdeen-Newcastle-Frankfurt scheduled service in a thirty-six-seat configuration, and at weekends one aircraft was converted to a fifty-seat layout for a Saturday service between Dundee and Jersey on behalf of Channel Island Travel.

In 1998 Brymon began operating the former British Airways Regional routes from Aberdeen to Manchester and Birmingham under a franchise agreement using Dash Eight aircraft. The Dash Sevens were retained for the oil charter contract work, with two examples being based at Aberdeen.

On 28 March 2002 Brymon Airways was merged with British Regional Airlines to form British Airways CitiExpress.

HIGHLAND AIRWAYS

Originally established in 1991 as Air Alba, and operating initially as a flying school, Highland Airways adopted its present name in March 1997. Based at Inverness, the airline is 95 per cent owned by Atlantic Holdings and is a sister company of Air Atlantique. One of its first major breakthroughs came with the award of a five-year contract from the Scottish Fisheries Protection Agency for reconnaissance flights using two Cessna 406 aircraft. From 1998 charter flights were operated on behalf of the oil industry from Aberdeen to such destinations as Cork, Waterford, Shannon, Newquay, Kristiansund, Farsund, Stavanger and Bergen. It was in 1998 that the newspaper industry relocated its distribution centre for the Scottish islands to Inverness and awarded Highland Airways a contract for daily flights from Inverness to Orkney, Shetland and Stornoway. Two aircraft were dedicated to these operations. From 1998 corporate shuttle flights were operated on behalf of BAE Systems Corporate Travel, using eighteen-seat Jetstream 31 turbo-props. Three or four services each week linked Glasgow and Filton, and the Jetstreams were also utilised at weekends to ferry flight crews between Glasgow, Liverpool and Teesside for the Airtours holiday group.

During the summer of 2001 a leased Portuguese Dornier 228 was operated out of Aberdeen on oil-related charters to Ireland, and in September of that year Highland Airways began scheduled services between Inverness, Stornoway and Benbecula. The Stornoway-Benbecula portion of these flights was operated under a Public Service Obligation contract for the Western Isles Council. These contracts were provided for under the Highlands and

Highland Airways Jetstream 31 G-JURA at Aberdeen in May 2003. *(Author)*

Islands Air Services (Scotland) Act of 1980, which made subsidies available to meet the deficits incurred by airlines providing socially necessary 'lifeline' services to the Scottish Highlands and Islands. Every weekday, one morning and one evening service were operated by Jetstream 31s under the 'Island Hopper Service' banner. The standard adult round trip fare between Inverness and Benbecula was £170, and between Stornoway and Benbecula the fare was £116 return.

By the summer of 2003 Highland Airways was also operating between Glasgow and Stornoway, and the initial ATR42 equipment on the route was replaced by leased Aerocondor Shorts 360 CS-TMY. On 4 September 2006 a new direct Inverness–Benbecula service was launched to complement the lunchtime connection via Stornoway, and every day except Friday a morning flight between Sumburgh and Inverness was provided. The staff complement now stood at seventy-one and the fleet included three Jetstream 31s and a Cessna 406 based at Inverness, and a freighter Shorts 360 stationed at Glasgow.

On 8 May 2007 Highland Airways began operating a new scheduled service between Cardiff and Anglesey (RAF Valley) in Wales. Eighteen-seater Jetstream 31s provided two round trips each weekday, under the terms of the first Public Service Obligation Contract to be issued in Wales. On 6 July 2007 Highland Airways carried its 2,000th passenger on this route. The fleet now comprised five Jetstream 31s and three Cessna 406s, two of which were operating for the Scottish Fisheries Protection Agency. In the summer of 2007 the airline

Highland Airways Jetstream 31 G-BTXG at Inverness on 16 August 2001. *(L.F. Sarjeant)*

Highland Airways Jetstream 31 G-JURA at Aberdeen in May 2003. *(Author)*

achieved 'preferred bidder' status for proposed new air links for the Inner Hebrides. With a target start date of October 2007 the services were to link Coll, Colonsay and Tirre with Oban. The contract was duly awarded, with services due to commence in January 2008. BN-2 Islander G-SEIL was acquired to operate the route, and Highland Airways also purchased a Beech 1900D for ad hoc work.

Highland Airways Cessna 406 G-LEAF at Inverness on 22 March 2002. *(L.F. Sarjeant)*

A Highland Airways Cessna 404 at Sumburgh on a freight and mail service from Aberdeen and Inverness. *(Kieran Murray)*

HIGHLAND EXPRESS

Highland Express was launched in 1987 as the only airline offering direct scheduled services to North America from Prestwick, Birmingham and London (Stansted) airports. Early investors included the founder Randolph Fields and Richard Branson. Economy and business-class travel was to be offered, with all passengers being provided with free in-flight entertainment and a choice of hot meals, and children also received complimentary fun packs and ice cream. Business-class passengers travelled in sleeper seats, and enjoyed complimentary limousine or helicopter transfers and the use of their own lounges at the airports.

Boeing 747-123 G-HIHO was delivered on 25 March 1987, and the start-up date was set at 30 May. There were initially to be Prestwick-New York (Newark) services every day except Mondays and Saturdays. From 5 June the Tuesday, Thursday and Friday flights were to originate at Stansted, and from 14 June the Wednesday and Sunday services would start from Birmingham. Schedules from Birmingham and Stansted to Toronto were due to begin a week or so later. There was to be an introductory economy-class fare of £99 one-way from any UK departure point to either New York or Toronto, while the business-class fare was set at £395 each way.

In the event, the services to New York did not commence until 4 July 1987, and the Toronto service was destined never to start. The Birmingham departures to New York were soon dropped, and during the autumn and winter of 1987–8 the New York flights only operated from Prestwick. An agreement was negotiated with British Caledonian Airways for the lease of BAC One-Eleven aircraft to provide a London-Prestwick connection, but this never actually started. The problems inherent in trying to provide a regular, reliable service with just one aircraft soon surfaced. In July 1987 one passenger complained to the *New York Times* that his flight from Stansted on 23 July had been delayed for 7 hours. Whilst at the airport he met another passenger who had been waiting three days for a flight. The previous service had been cancelled as the aircraft was still in Brussels, undergoing maintenance with the Belgian carrier SABENA.

In November 1987 Highland Express defaulted on a $3 million payment instalment to the finance company Citicorp, and on 11 December 1987 the airline was declared bankrupt. The Boeing 747 was impounded at Brussels, but later renewed its association with Richard Branson as G-VMIA of Virgin Atlantic.

FLYWHOOSH

Flywhoosh commenced operations on 29 May 2007 from Dundee to Birmingham and Belfast City Airport. The carrier was an affiliate of the Polish charter airline White Eagle, whose ATR 42 turbo-prop aircraft was used. However, disagreements between the two airlines led to White Eagle withdrawing its aircraft, and operations were suspended on 7 December 2007.

MALINAIR

In June 1985, Glasgow lawyer Frank Cannon formed Malinair, and in December of that year scheduled services between Glasgow and Carrickfinn commenced with two Islander aircraft. Ambitious expansion plans led to the recruitment of a number of former Air Ecosse staff, including Malinair's new general manager and operations manager.

In the summer of 1986 the former Air Ecosse route from Aberdeen to Belfast via Glasgow was taken over by Malinair and operated initially on Air Ecosse's licence under the flight prefix WG with leased Dornier 228 equipment.

For the summer of 1987 Malinair had three Islanders and three Dornier 228s in use on a mixture of night mail operations and daytime scheduled passenger services. The latter included four round trips each weekday between Glasgow and Belfast, with two of them originating at Aberdeen. The Dorniers were also used on Manchester-Donegal and Glasgow-Teeside-Gatwick schedules, and for a short time a Glasgow-Humberside route was operated with Islander equipment, but on 19 June 1987 Malinair ceased operations.

AIR CALEDONIAN

Air Caledonian was established in 2003 as a wholly-owned subsidiary of Clasair, based at Prestwick. Operations commenced on 6 December 2004 with flights to the Scottish islands being carried out by a single Bandeirante aircraft, but were suspended in January 2005.

British Eagle Dove G-AROI *Eaglet*, used on feeder services between Dundee and Glasgow. *(Air-Britain)*

BRITISH EAGLE

In July 1966 British Eagle International Airlines opened a feeder service between Dundee and Glasgow to provide connections with the airline's trunk route flights from Glasgow to London (Heathrow). De Havilland Dove G-AROI 'Eaglet' maintained this link until the service was suspended on 30 September 1967, primarily because Autair had been granted approval for Dundee-Carlisle-Heathrow services.

MACAIR

Macair commenced operations in April 1995, and used two Jetstream aircraft (on lease from the Scandinavian airline Sun Air) on services linking Edinburgh and Birmingham with Carrickfinn and Londonderry. The airline ceased operations on 26 June 1995, blaming its failure partly on the bankruptcy of its sales agent, Total Mobility of Ware, Hertfordshire.

Air Orkney Islander G-BESO at Inverness on 6 September 1984. *(L.F. Sarjeant)*

Air Orkney Islander G-AXXG at Inverness on 5 April 1983 after its Cairngorms mishap. *(L.F. Sarjeant)*

AIR ORKNEY

In 1981 an Orkney businessman established Air Orkney as an air charter company. The airline's first chief pilot was former Loganair pilot Andy Alsop, but in 1983 he left for a flying job in the Falkland Islands and his place was taken by Ed Bewley. During its first year of operations Air Orkney completed 273 charter contracts, involving 791 landings. 2,828 passengers were carried, and the aircraft visited nearly fifty airfields throughout the Scottish islands and mainland.

On 21 March 1983 Islander aircraft G-AXXH operated a charter flight from Wick to Fair Isle. After dropping off his passenger there the pilot landed at Eday to dip his fuel tanks. He estimated that he had enough fuel to get to Kirkwall, and landed there without any problems. However, when the aircraft was refuelled there it was discovered that there was less than 1 kg of fuel left in the tanks. This was the result of a mix-up between litres and kilos when the previous load of fuel had been uplifted. Three days later the airline's first aircraft, Islander G-AXXG, ran out of fuel and crash-landed on the top of Carn Sleamhuin in the Cairngorms. It was replaced by Islander G-BESO, which was leased to Loganair in June 1984. Air Orkney ceased operations that year.

CHIEFTAIN AIRWAYS

In 1986 Glasgow-based Ace Aviation was awarded licences to operate from Glasgow to Brussels, Gothenburg and Hamburg, and from Edinburgh to Brussels, Copenhagen, Frankfurt and Milan from June of that year. To operate these services the company changed its name to ACE Scottish European Airways and announced its intention to use Beech King Air 200s, but no such services under this name took place and the licences were acquired by Chieftain Airways.

Operations by Chieftain Airways commenced on 29 March 1987, with two weekday round trips from Glasgow to Brussels via Edinburgh using HS748 turbo-prop aircraft, and one round trip from Glasgow to Hamburg with an eight-seater King Air. The fare from Glasgow or Edinburgh to Brussels was £215 return, and from Glasgow to Hamburg it was £186 return. During the summer of 1987 Chieftain Airways also intended to introduce services from Glasgow to Gothenburg and Geneva and from Edinburgh to Copenhagen and Milan, but before these could be realised the airline ceased operations on 13 May 1987.

SCOTTISH EUROPEAN AIRWAYS

Scottish European Airways commenced services from Glasgow to Brussels and Frankfurt on 14 November 1988, using the two former Chieftain Airways HS748 aircraft. For the summer of 1989 there was one weekday round trip between Glasgow and Brussels, the outbound leg routeing via Edinburgh and the return leg operating non-stop. Frankfurt was served by one daily round trip from Glasgow which called at Newcastle en route. On Sundays there was an

Scottish European HS748 G-BPDA at Edinburgh in September 1989. *(Author)*

Scottish European Airways HS748 G-BPFU. *(Air-Britain)*

additional service via Edinburgh and Newcastle, and from Edinburgh there was a weekday round trip via Brussels.

The routes were scheduled to continue throughout the winter of 1989–90, and plans were announced to upgrade many of the schedules to BAC One-Eleven jet equipment for the coming summer. However, early in 1990 one HS748 was impounded at Manchester and the other was grounded at Frankfurt. Services continued erratically, using leased aircraft, but by the end of April 1990 all flying had ceased.

DIRECTFLIGHT

In 1992 Bedfordshire-based Directflight gained a contract from the Scottish Fisheries Protection Agency to provide offshore aerial surveillance flights, using two modified Cessna F406 aircraft based at Prestwick. The contract was renewed in 1996, extended in 2002 and completed in 2004.

From 1 August 2006 Directflight took over the Loganair schedules from Tingwall to Fair Isle, Foula, Papa Stour and The Skerries, using a new Islander aircraft purchased by the Shetland Islands Council and leased to them for the services.

Directflight took over the Shetland inter-island services from Loganair on 1 August 2006. Islander G-SICB is illustrated. *(Kieran Murray)*

BURNTHILL HELICOPTERS

In 1978 JetRanger helicopter G-BAKT was purchased and used to start scheduled services from Glasgow to Fort William. The helicopter was based at Hangar 12 at Glasgow and operated morning and afternoon schedules to Fort William Heliport, timed to connect with British Airways flights from Heathrow to Glasgow and British Caledonian services from Gatwick. The single fare cost £25 and the flight duration was around 40 minutes.

For the first year the service was subsidised to the tune of £24,000 by the Highlands and Islands Development Board and various local authorities. The subsidies continued on an annual basis, although disagreements caused most of the local authorities to drop out, leaving the HIDB to bear the brunt of the costs. During 1982 and 1983 schedules were flown from the Glasgow base to Fort William, Rothesay, Lochgilphead and Oban with JetRanger equipment, and services also operated from Rothesay Pier to destinations in the Argylle area in the mid-1980s. Burnthill Helicopters was bought by Air Charter Scotland in May 1983, but continued operations using JetRangers G-BAKT and G-WOSP until early 1985.

EASTERN AIRWAYS

Although at first glance Humberside-based Eastern Airways may seem to be an unusual choice for inclusion in a book on Scotland's airlines, the carrier is now the second busiest airline at Aberdeen Airport (after British Airways and its franchise operators), and it was from a Humberside-Aberdeen route that the present extensive network was grown. Twice-daily services began in December 1997 with a single leased Metro III turbo-prop registered TF-BBG. For the summer of 1998 the frequency had been increased to three round trips each weekday, although the fleet still stood at just one aircraft.

By the summer of 1999 Jetstream 32 aircraft had been introduced into service, although the flight schedules remained the same. The gradual withdrawal of KLM UK from its routes up the east coast of England to Aberdeen gave Eastern Airways the opportunity to step in and take over this network. From 7 February 2000 Eastern operated two round trips each weekday between Aberdeen and Norwich, and a similar frequency on the route from Glasgow to Norwich via Humberside. There was also a short-lived weekday service between Aberdeen and Haugesund in Norway. The summer of 2001 saw the introduction of morning and evening weekday flights from Aberdeen to Wick, and three weekday round trips between Aberdeen and the East Midlands.

Eastern Airways Jetstream 31 G-BUVC at Inverness on 2 August 2003. *(L.F. Sarjeant)*

Major fleet expansion came in 2002 when Eastern Airways acquired the British Airways CitiExpress fleet of twelve Jetstream 41s and its engineering hangar at Glasgow Airport. In subsequent years further Jetstream 41s were purchased in the USA. New routes continued to open. In the summer of 2003 a Monday-Friday Aberdeen-Belfast schedule was introduced, along with two Aberdeen-Newcastle-Southampton flights each weekday. Leased Embraer 135 regional jets were added to the fleet, but were soon disposed of in favour of more turbo-prop aircraft. These included fifty-seat Saab 2000s, which were used to launch direct Aberdeen-Southampton flights in March 2005, complementing the existing services via Newcastle.

Jetstream 31 G-EEST was written off at Wick on 17 September 2003, fortunately without injury to the four passengers and three crew on the scheduled service from Aberdeen. The aircraft crossed the threshold of runway 31 at Wick, flying 21 knots faster than the recommended approach speed. It floated at 6ft above the runway then bounced twice, the second time with sufficient force to crack the wing spar and allow the right-hand propeller to come into contact with the runway. It then bounced again before finally landing.

On 9 January 2006 Eastern Airways began a weekday service between Aberdeen and Stornoway with support from the Scottish Executive's Route Development Fund. From 20 March Aberdeen-Norwich flights were upgraded from Jetstream 41 to Saab 2000 equipment, in a bid to counter the introduction of jet aircraft on the route by competitor BMI Commuter.

In April 2006 one of the Saab 2000s was unveiled in new 'Aberdeen, City and Shire' promotional livery, which it carried initially on Aberdeen-Newcastle-Southampton flights. The withdrawal of Air Wales from scheduled service operations that month enabled Eastern to take over its Aberdeen-Cardiff schedules on 24 April with Jetstream 41s, and the same aircraft type was used to launch Inverness-Leeds/Bradford schedules on that same date.

From May 2006 eligible passengers on the Aberdeen-Wick and Aberdeen-Stornoway routes could travel at reduced rates under the Scottish Executive's Air Discount Scheme. This provided a 40 per cent discount on air fares for people whose main residence was in Orkney, Shetland, the Western Isles, Islay, Jura, Caithness or north-west Sutherland. It was intended to enable residents of the remoter parts of Scotland to enjoy the benefits of affordable air travel and to increase their access to further education. Those eligible included students from these areas who were studying away from home and travelling to another airport within the areas or to Glasgow, Edinburgh, Aberdeen or Inverness. There was no restriction on the number of discounted trips that could be made.

Expansion at Inverness continued in 2006. On 5 June Jetstream 41 flights between Inverness and Newcastle were launched, adding to the existing services from Inverness to Leeds/Bradford, Birmingham, Manchester and Southampton, and in November new Saturday flights to Manchester and Birmingham were added.

On 3 October 2006 the six occupants of a scheduled service from Aberdeen to Wick had a lucky escape when their Jetstream 31 almost touched down at Wick with the undercarriage

Eastern Airways Jetstream 31 G-CBDA at Inverness on 20 February 2004. *(L.F. Sarjeant)*

still retracted. Although debris from the fuselage belly pod and strike marks from the propellers were found on the runway at Wick the pilot was able to get the aircraft airborne again and returned safely to Aberdeen.

From 12 February 2007 the Aberdeen-Wick and Aberdeen-Stornoway services were upgraded to Jetstream 41 equipment, and three round trips were scheduled for each weekday. During 2007 Eastern Airways was operating 138 services each week from Aberdeen, and employed thirty-two staff there. Destinations included Newcastle, Norwich, Southampton, Teeside, Humberside, East Midlands, Leeds/Bradford, Bristol, Stornoway and Wick. All passengers could take advantage of the Eastern Airways lounge at Aberdeen, regardless of the fare paid.

On 13 August 2007 Eastern Airways added its first international route, from Aberdeen to Stavanger, to the ten routes already operated. Fifty-seat Saab 2000s flew morning and evening round trips each weekday.

AIR ANGLIA

Air Anglia was formed in July 1970 by the merger of three East Anglia-based charter companies. One of these, Rig-Air, had previously been using Dakotas on oil-related charter work. Air Anglia commenced charter operations in August 1970, with regular charters out of Norwich for the oil industry. These included flights to Aberdeen, and on

7 December the airline inaugurated its first scheduled service, from Norwich to Edinburgh and onwards to Aberdeen with Islander aircraft. In 1971 two more Dakotas were acquired and in March of that year an office was opened at Aberdeen Airport. On 5 May 1971 Dakota flights from Aberdeen to Sumburgh for Shell began, and similar charters were also operated for Esso. By 1973 two Dakotas were based at Aberdeen for oil-related charters.

Scheduled service expansion took place during 1972, with the opening of a Norwich-Teesside-Aberdeen route on 5 June, and also Norwich-Newcastle-Aberdeen services. Fokker F-27 turbo-prop equipment was introduced onto the latter route on 6 September 1972. In June 1972 an application for an Aberdeen-Kirkwall-Sumburgh scheduled service had been lodged with the Civil Aviation Authority, but this had been rejected.

On 20 November 1973 Dakota G-AGJV, on an oil charter from Sumburgh to Aberdeen with thirty-two passengers aboard, developed a hydraulic leak en route, but made a safe emergency landing at Aberdeen.

For 1974 one Dakota and a Piper Aztec aircraft were stationed at Aberdeen for cargo flights and charter work, but the major expansion was in the field of scheduled services. On 1 April Aberdeen-Amsterdam and Aberdeen-Stavanger passenger services were inaugurated, followed by Norwich-Leeds/Bradford-Edinburgh-Aberdeen services on 6 May. All these new routes utilised F-27 equipment, as did an Aberdeen-Bergen route opened on 31 August 1975. All-cargo Dakota services Aberdeen and Amsterdam commenced on 10 May 1975. During the summer of 1975 Air Anglia offered package holidays from Aberdeen to the Italian Adriatic through its associate company, Anglia Holidays. Passengers first flew to Amsterdam on the scheduled service, and enjoyed a night-stop there which included a sightseeing canal cruise as part of the package. They then boarded a Caravelle jet for the onward flight to Rimini. On 24 November 1975 the last Dakota aircraft was retired and Argosy turbo-prop freighters took over the Aberdeen-Amsterdam cargo services. Initially these aircraft were leased from Air Bridge Carriers, but on 6 December 1975 Air Anglia took delivery of Argosy G-APRL, on a twelve-month lease from Field Aircraft Services and wearing full Air Anglia livery.

By January 1976 Air Anglia was operating scheduled services from Aberdeen to Amsterdam, Bergen, Stavanger, Norwich, Newcastle, Teesside, Leeds/Bradford and Edinburgh, and all-cargo services to Amsterdam and Norwich. On 1 April 1976 Humberside Airport was added to the list of passenger destinations. Fokker F-28 jets were introduced onto the schedules from Aberdeen on 8 August 1978. During the winter of 1979–80 they were in use on Aberdeen-Edinburgh-Amsterdam services (three round trips each weekday) and Aberdeen-Edinburgh-Paris (Orly) and Aberdeen-Stavanger schedules. Turbo-prop F-27s operated to Bergen, Edinburgh, Newcastle, Teesside, Humberside, Leeds/Bradford, London (Stansted) and Norwich.

On 1 January 1980 Air Anglia was merged with British Island Airways to form Air UK, which continued to develop the route network from Aberdeen.

LOCH LOMOND SEAPLANES

Based in Helensburgh, Argyll, Loch Lomond Seaplanes was formed in January 2003 and launched a programme of excursion and charter services in the spring of 2004. The company is owned and operated by Captain David West, a commercial pilot with over twenty-five-years' experience. The fleet in 2007 comprised a six-seater Cessna 206 and a ten-seater Cessna 208 Caravan, both float-equipped. On 20 August 2007 the company operated a special inaugural flight from Glasgow to Oban for the media. Regular flights on the route from a terminal on the River Clyde near the Glasgow Science Centre were due to commence after Christmas 2007, with a fare of £149 one-way. Regular flights to Mull, Arran and Bute were also to be offered, and the company was considering the possibility of extending the Oban service to Skye.

CHAPTER SIX

OIL-RELATED CHARTERS

During the 1970s the search for oil and gas beneath the North Sea, and the construction of oil rigs, pipelines and shore-based installations to process it, led to an unprecedented increase in aircraft and helicopter movements at Scottish airports, and at Aberdeen Airport in particular. Many new charter companies came into existence to service the oil boom, and established operators such as Dan-Air based substantial numbers of aircraft at Aberdeen to fulfil contracts with the oil companies. Today the exploration phase of the North Sea oil industry is virtually over, but the legacy of the 1970s lives on in the greatly expanded airport facilities and the network of scheduled services linking the international offices of oil companies. Here are some of the companies whose expansion (and in most cases decline and collapse) centred around the 'black gold'.

PETERS AVIATION

On 19 March 1973 de Havilland Heron G-APKW arrived at Aberdeen to open a base there for oil-related charter work. By the end of the year two more Herons were based there. One was subsequently sent on detachment to Dundee to operate flights for Conoco. In the spring of 1975 the airline was awarded a contract for the use of two Dakotas out of Aberdeen for Mobil Oil, but the oil companies soon began to insist on more modern turbo-prop equipment for their flights and Peters Aviation ceased operations shortly afterwards.

MACEDONIAN AVIATION

Macedonian Aviation Dakota G-AMPO arrived at Aberdeen Airport on 31 December 1973 to operate a two-week programme of oil-related charter flights. On 27 April 1974 it was joined by sister-ship G-AMHJ, and the two Dakotas were primarily used on charters between Aberdeen and Sumburgh. Macedonian had hopes of acquiring turbo-prop equipment to satisfy the demands of its client companies, and opened negotiations for the purchase of either six ex-Air Canada Viscounts or three former Eastern Provincial Airways Heralds, but the finance was not forthcoming and on 6 November the Dakotas were ferried back to Southend and the airline ceased operations.

SITE AVIATION

In January 1974 Site Aviation leased three Viscount 800s from British Midland Airways and based them at Aberdeen for oil-related charters within Scotland and to Scandinavian cities. These flights continued until the end of April 1974 when the company ran into financial difficulties. Operations ceased in May 1974.

AIR BRIDGE CARRIERS

In July 1974 cargo specialist Air Bridge Carriers based an Argosy freighter at Aberdeen for four months to carry out a series of charters to Rotterdam.

ALIDAIR/INTER-CITY AIRLINES

Alidair was formed in January 1972 as a subsidiary of Alida Packaging, and went on to set up its own subsidiaries, Alidair Scotland and Guernsey Airlines. In February 1975 a Viscount was sent to Aberdeen to commence operating charters to Sumburgh, Bergen, Stavanger, Norwich and Amsterdam on behalf of Burmah Oil and Total Oil. A weekly flight to Bergen was also operated for Shell (Norway). In May 1975 a small fleet of ex-Air Inter Viscount 700s was acquired, and these proved ideal for the long flights from Sumburgh direct to Heathrow that were being operated for the oil industry. For the summer of 1975 Alidair had two Viscounts stationed at Aberdeen, operating on behalf of six oil-related companies. Most of the flights were from Sumburgh or Aberdeen to Scandinavian destinations, but the airline also operated a service from Edinburgh to Düsseldorf and back each Thursday.

On 25 October 1979 Guernsey Airlines Viscount G-BFYZ was operating an oil charter to Kirkwall when it overran the runway after touchdown; luckily there were no serious injuries.

In October 1980 Alidair began operating a scheduled service from Edinburgh to East Midlands and Brussels under the name of Inter-City Airlines. This was followed by the inauguration of another scheduled service from Aberdeen to the East Midlands via Edinburgh on 1 April 1981, using Viscount and Shorts 330 aircraft. The Edinburgh-East Midlands-Brussels service was later withdrawn because of poor passenger demand. During the summer of 1981 Guernsey Airlines operated Viscount services from Prestwick to Jersey at weekends.

On 1 January 1983 Alidair commenced a major new contract for Aberdeen-Sumburgh services for Shell. From 28 March that year Aberdeen and Edinburgh were also linked to Jersey, with a Viscount flying Aberdeen-Jersey-Edinburgh-Jersey-Aberdeen each Saturday for the summer season. On weekdays a Shorts 330 operated an East Midlands-Edinburgh-Aberdeen-Edinburgh-East Midlands schedule, with a day return fare of £40 on offer between Edinburgh and Aberdeen. On 4 July 1983, however, Alidair and Inter-City Airlines ceased operations, Guernsey Airlines having been sold to British Air Ferries a short time before.

DAN-AIR

In early 1974 the long-established charter and scheduled service airline Dan-Air began its association with Aberdeen Airport by basing an HS748 there for oil-support charter work. By September of that year Dan-Air had established a base at Aberdeen, and a contract was obtained from Conoco for flights between Aberdeen and Sumburgh. Other charters were operated from Aberdeen and Edinburgh to Amsterdam, Bergen. Esbjerg, Kristiansand, Oslo and Rotterdam. During 1974 and 1975 a weekly crew change flight from Aberdeen to Oporto was carried out for the owners of the Transworld 61 rig off the coast of Portugal. The influx of oil workers to Aberdeen, and the increase in prosperity in the area, provided Dan-Air with opportunities to open new holiday routes, and for the summer of 1975 HS748 scheduled services were operated between Aberdeen and the Isle of Man. These were followed in October 1975 by a series of weekly Comet 4 inclusive tour flights to Palma.

On 27 July 1977 Dan-Air opened a new operations and engineering complex at Aberdeen on the site of the former fire station on the east side of the airport. In July 1977 there were five HS748s based at Aberdeen, and the airline stated its intention to increase this figure to ten by the end of the summer. At the peak of the oil boom Dan-Air had fourteen HS748s allocated to its Oil Support Division. Eight aircraft were based at Aberdeen, three at Scatsta in Shetland, one at Glasgow and two rotating between Teesside and Aberdeen. The North Sea oil industry was spending around £2 million each day on all forms of transportation, including aircraft and helicopters. Dan-Air was operating over sixty flights every day, with six aircraft on hire to Shell Exploration and Production, one allocated to Unionoil, and four to Foster-Wheeler/BP for the Sullom Voe Oil Terminal construction project in Shetland.

Dan-Air HS748 G-BFLL at Aberdeen in April 1990. *(Author)*

Special dispensation had been given for Dan-Air's HS748s to use Scatsta's Category D-width runway, which was far too narrow for the Viscounts of British Air Ferries, Dan-Air's main competitor. These had to operate into Sumburgh, on the southern tip of the island. When the Sullom Voe workforce was repatriated for the Christmas/Hogmanay break, additional HS748s had to be drafted in to assist the operation of around 100 flights to the Scottish mainland and then back again at the end of the holiday period. On 8 January 1978 there were no less than nine Dan-Air HS748s present at Glasgow Airport.

On 31 July 1979 Dan-Air HS748 series 1 G-BEKF was taking off from Sumburgh on an oil charter with forty-four passengers and three crew aboard, when it failed to become airborne and ran into the sea at the end of the runway. Fifteen passengers and two crew members lost their lives. The accident investigation found that the aircraft's elevators were locked, and concluded that the elevator gust locks had probably been re-engaged during the pre-flight checks.

In 1979 Dan-Air was awarded a licence for Aberdeen-London (Gatwick) scheduled services using BAC One-Eleven jets. At the end of March 1983 the Inverness-London (Heathrow) route was taken over from British Airways, again using One-Eleven equipment. Thirty staff were employed at Inverness to handle the scheduled services and also charter flights.

By then, the heyday of the oil-related charter work had passed, although Dan-Air still had six HS748s engaged on this type of activity.

British World ATP G-OBWO at Aberdeen in June 2000. *(Author)*

Dan-Air HS748 G-BEJD at Inverness in March 1983 with a British Airways S-61N helicopter behind. *(Iain Sarjeant)*

BRITISH AIR FERRIES/BRITISH WORLD AIRLINES

In the aftermath of the collapse of Alidair and Inter City Airlines on 4 July 1983, the Shell Expro contract for flights between Aberdeen and Sumburgh was taken over by Southend-based British Air Ferries. Initially a Viscount 700 leased from the Receiver of Alidair was used, and the same aircraft carried out operations to repatriate stranded passengers who were booked to return from Jersey on the Alidair scheduled services, but this aircraft operated its last service on 30 September 1983 and was replaced by British Air Ferries Viscount 800s. A fleet of three was based at Aberdeen, two to operate the daily Shell charters and one in reserve. When Aberdeen Airport staged an Air Travel Day on 21 January 1984, British Air Ferries operated local pleasure flights with a seventy-six-seater Viscount at a price of £8 per head.

In 1988 cash flow problems forced British Air Ferries into administration, but services were maintained, and with the support of Shell and other major customers the airline emerged from administration on 3 May 1989. On 6 April 1993 the company was renamed British World Airlines. The Shell charters to Sumburgh continued, and during the summer of 1993 Viscounts were also used on a Royal Mail Parcelforce contract for flights between Edinburgh and Coventry on weeknights.

The Shell contract was put out to tender again in 1995 and British World fought off competition from Gill Airways and other operators to win a five-year renewal valued at

BWA Viscount G-BFZL in the airline's final colour scheme at Edinburgh in 1994. *(Author)*

A British World Airways BAe 146 in March 1996. *(Kieran Murray)*

British World Airways Viscount 806 G-APEY departs from Sumburgh for Aberdeen. *(Kieran Murray)*

British Air Ferries
Viscount 802 G-AOHM
taxiing. *(British Air Ferries)*

A pair of British Air
Ferries on the Shell
contract at Aberdeen
in 1994.

British World Viscount
807 G-CSZB performs
a flypast along runway
15/33 at Sumburgh
before operating the last
Viscount-operated Shell
charter to Aberdeen.
(Kieran Murray)

British World Viscount 807 G-CSZB at Sumburgh after a Shell charter from Aberdeen in 1995. *(Author)*

British World's second ATR72 G-OILB at Aberdeen in 1996. *(Author)*

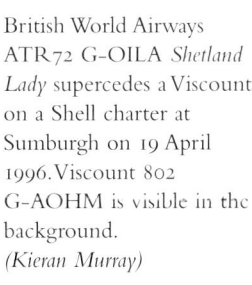

British World Airways ATR72 G-OILA *Shetland Lady* supercedes a Viscount on a Shell charter at Sumburgh on 19 April 1996. Viscount 802 G-AOHM is visible in the background.
(Kieran Murray)

$88 million. Viscount 802 G-AOHM, Viscount 806 G-APEY and Viscount 807 G-CSZB were stationed at Aberdeen to fulfil the contract, which had already seen around 1.5 million passengers carried to and from Sumburgh.

The faithful Viscounts were eventually retired from passenger service in 1996 and were replaced on the Shell contract flights by ATR72-210 and ATP turbo-props. The first ATR72, G-OILA, replaced one of the Viscounts in April 1996, and the plan was for the other two Viscounts to share the load with it until the second example was delivered in late May. However, such was the reliability of G-OILA that it proved itself able to operate the programme of flights single-handedly and the second aircraft, G-OILB, after an initial spell at Aberdeen, went on lease to City Flyer Express for thirty months instead.

In February 2000 British World was awarded a contract by Bristow Helicopters for the provision of flights for their staff from Aberdeen to Scatsta in Shetland, before transfer to Bristow Helicopters for their onward journey to the rigs. To cope with the additional workload an additional fifteen staff were taken on at Aberdeen Airport. By 2001 four ATP turbo-props were based at Aberdeen, but on 29 November a dispute over allegedly unpaid airport charges resulted in them being impounded there. Urgent negotiations with the British Airports Authority secured the release of three of them in time to operate the following day's flying programme, and the fourth example was released shortly afterwards. The impounding incident, which also involved a British World Boeing 737 jet at Stansted Airport, came some weeks after the airline's staff had reportedly had payment of 15 per cent of their salaries deferred until August 2002, and on 14 December 2001 British World Airlines ceased operations and went into receivership. At the time there were around fifty staff employed at Aberdeen Airport.

FLIGHTLINE

Flightline was originally formed at Southend Airport in April 1989 as an aircraft broker and charter operator with Bandeirante and King Air turbo-props. It acquired its first BAe 146 jet in March 1993, and in December 2001 it was able to use this type to take over the Aberdeen-Shetland contract at short notice from the failed British World Airlines. In 2002 the temporary contract was firmed up and extended for three more years. It called for the operation of BAe 146 flights on behalf of the Integrated Oil Consortium, and won in the face of competition from BAC Express (using former British World ATPs) and Atlantic Airways of the Faroe Islands (using BAe 146s). Three aircraft were dedicated to the flights and the aircraft attracted a very favourable response from its passengers. In early 2004 the contract for flights to Scatsta was extended for a further three years, commencing 1 July 2005.

Flightline BAe 146 G-TBIC in IAC livery, taxiing at Aberdeen in May 2003. *(Author)*

Flightline BAe 146 G-DEFL at Scatsta in December 2003. Its sister aircraft, G-FLTA, is in the background. *(Kieran Murray)*

Before acquiring BAe 146 jets, Flightline operated smaller aircraft on charters. This picture shows Bandeirante G-FLTY at Aberdeen in 1993. *(Author)*

CHAPTER SEVEN

SCOTTISH AIR AMBULANCE SERVICES

Until recently air ambulance flights within Scotland were provided by the scheduled service airlines as an extension of their normal commercial activities, and were initially operated on an ad hoc basis. The first official air ambulance flight in Scotland took place on 14 May 1933. John McDermid, a thirty-three-year-old fisherman on Islay, was suffering from perforation of the stomach and there was a real risk of peritonitis setting in. The attending doctor sent a telegram to the St Andrews Ambulance Association requesting an airlift to the mainland. Captain J.H. Orrell of Midland and Scottish Air Ferries flew out in DH84 Dragon G-ACCZ, landing on the sands near Bridgend. On the return flight to Glasgow the patient was accompanied by Mrs A.W. Ferguson, a nurse from Glasgow who happened to be on holiday on Islay at the time. The first air ambulance flight to Skye followed on 19 July 1933 after a Dr Fothergill had been taken ill whilst on holiday in Uig. Again it was Midland and Scottish Air Ferries that provided the aircraft, flying the patient through a violent thunderstorm to Edinburgh for transfer to the Royal Infirmary.

In October 1934 Highland Airways was awarded a contract by Orkney County Council for the provision of air ambulance services between the Northern Isles and Balfour Hospital on the Orkney mainland. The contract was later extended to cover the carriage of urgent medical cases from Orkney to Aberdeen. In January 1935 the contract was taken over by Northern and Scottish Airways. Aberdeen Airways operated its first air ambulance flight on 2 February 1936, when Captain Eric Starling took DH84 Dragon G-ADFI to St Margarets Hope on South Ronaldsay to pick up a patient bound for Stromness and onwards to the Balfour Hospital. After landing he needed two helpers to grab a wingtip each to prevent the aircraft from blowing over. The first air ambulance flight from Shetland was to airlift

Gama Aviation King Air 200 G-SASC at Sumburgh in Scottish Ambulance Service colours on 1 July 2006. *(Kieran Murray)*

Alex MacRae, the keeper of the Esha Ness lighthouse, to Edinburgh on 30 April 1937. Northern Lighthouses chartered DH84 Dragon G-ACAN of Allied Airways for the flight, which used a grass strip about 50 yards from the lighthouse, the site having been cleared by Mr MacRae's son and daughter. The flight to Edinburgh took 4 hours. Another hazardous mission was carried out by Scottish Airways pilot John Hankins at the end of February 1939. He landed on Sanday in dark and stormy conditions with the aid of the headlights of two cars, which had been positioned so as to form an illuminated letter 'L' on the grass landing strip.

In November 1947 the National Health Service was set up to provide free healthcare in the UK, and responsibility for the funding of ambulance flights in Scotland passed from local communities to the Department of Health for Scotland (later to become the Scottish Home and Health Department). In February of that year the newly-formed British European Airways (BEA) began providing air ambulance services in Scotland. On 11 February 1948 Captain E.E. Fresson, then BEA manager for the Highlands and Islands and pioneer of pre-war services to Orkney, flew DH84 Dragon G-ACIT to Stronsay, Sanday, North Ronaldsay and Westray with three inspectors from the Ministry of Civil Aviation to evaluate possible landing grounds on the islands. Whilst on Westray he received an urgent request to airlift a seriously injured boy from Stronsay to the Balfour Hospital in Kirkwall. This he did, but he was then seriously rebuked by the BEA senior management for not obtaining prior authorisation for the flight. Within a fortnight he had received notice of redundancy, and he left BEA on 31 March 1948. By March 1948 BEA had completed 182 ambulance flights on an ad hoc basis, and in April of that year the airline set up a dedicated Air Ambulance

Unit at Glasgow Airport under the management of Captain David Barclay. Services were provided in conjunction with the Ministry of Civil Aviation and the Department of Health, and the initial aircraft complement was two DH89 Dragon Rapide aircraft, crewed by three pilots and three radio operators. Nurses were supplied on a volunteer basis as required by the Southern General Hospital in Glasgow. BEA had always shown reluctance to send aircraft to the smaller airstrips and had rejected two calls for ambulance flights out of Westray during one week in April 1948. The airline's anxiety was heightened on 15 January 1949 when DH89 Dragon Rapide G-AHXV was severely damaged when it overturned whilst landing on the waterlogged grass strip at North Ronaldsay.

In 1955 BEA took delivery of a de Havilland Heron aircraft for its Scottish network. The series 1 variant with a fixed undercarriage was chosen as this was thought to be better suited to landings on such surfaces as the cockle strand beach on Barra. The first Heron-operated air ambulance sortie took place on 4 March 1955 and the Herons went on to operate an average of around 250 such flights each year. Patients from Orkney and Shetland were usually flown to Aberdeen, whereas those from the Western Isles usually went to Glasgow or sometimes Inverness. For ambulance flights the Herons were equipped with two stretchers, oxygen and cots for babies. The annual operating cost of around £12,000 was met by the Scottish Health Service, and the volunteer nurses from Glasgow's Southern General Hospital were given additional training for this specialised duty. After completing ten air ambulance sorties each nurse was awarded a silver wings brooch, the only decoration not awarded by a nursing college that a nurse was permitted to wear on her uniform.

On 21 February 1956 Captain David Barclay managed the feat of completing three air ambulance missions in the space of 8 hours. At 1100hrs he took off from Renfrew and flew through a thunderstorm to Kirkwall to pick up a woman who needed hospitalisation in Aberdeen. On his way back to Renfrew he responded to a call to fly to Barra and collect an eighty-one-year-old woman who had fallen and broken her leg. On completion of this trip he was sent to Benbecula where a seventy-four-year-old man needed a transfer to Glasgow. When he finally landed at Renfrew at 1900hrs he had flown a total of 740 miles.

The hazardous nature of air ambulance work was underlined by two incidents in 1957. On 20 February Heron G-ANXA was damaged while landing at Coll. The aircraft was hit by a sudden crosswind and slid onto the rough ground, which removed the undercarriage, broke the main spar and flattened both starboard engines against the wing. The aircraft was repaired and put back into service but worse was to come. On 28 September the crew of Heron G-AOFY received a call to fly to Islay to pick up a shepherd's wife who was seriously ill. During the final approach in low cloud and poor visibility the aircraft's left wing struck the ground and the aircraft crashed, killing Captain T.N. Calderwood, Radio Officer Hugh McGinlay and Sister Jean Kennedy, who had completed over 200 air ambulance flights. When news of the crash came through to Renfrew a second Heron was prepared and despatched under the command of Captain Eric Starling. It was dawn before they were able to uplift the patient, but sadly she died during the approach to Renfrew. Heron G-ANXA was renamed *Sister Jean Kennedy*, and a cairn was later erected at Renfrew near the site of the airport to pay tribute to all the airmen and nurses who served the Scottish Air Ambulance Service from 1933 until the airport closed in 1966. A separate plaque on the cairn remembers the crew of G-AOFY.

Captain David Barclay was awarded the MBE in recognition of his work with the Air Ambulance Unit, and on 29 February 1960 he was the subject of a *This Is Your Life* television programme. Among those taking part was Jimmy Mitchell, who had been Captain Barclay's radio officer with Scottish Airways and had served with BEA at Renfrew as flight administration officer since 1949, finally retiring from BEA in 1965.

During the financial year 1962/3 the Air Ambulance Unit transported 350 patients. On some occasions, when a Heron was not available, a Handley Page Herald turbo-prop was substituted.

On 16 June 1967 Loganair operated its first air ambulance flight, from Oronsay to Glasgow with Piper Aztec G-ASYB under the command of Captain Ken Foster. BEA Herons continued to serve seven Scottish airfields, with Loganair operating their Islanders in a supplementary role to the smaller airstrips, beginning with Coll, Oronsay, Mull and Oban. In May 1968 BEA's Captain Eric Starling flew fifteen-year-old Alex Smith from Lewis to Edinburgh after he had accidentally drunk weedkiller from a lemonade bottle. Alex underwent Europe's first lung transplant during his treatment at Edinburgh Royal Infirmary.

At the end of March 1973 British Airways (which BEA had become part of) retired its Herons and handed over responsibility for the Scottish Air Ambulance flights to Loganair. During the next ten years Loganair was to carry almost 10,000 patients. Its first international sortie came in June 1973 when a Norwegian seaman was crushed by a ship docking in Stromness and was flown from Kirkwall to Bergen. In 1976 Loganair made a special award of a pair of gold 'wings' to Gisela Elisabeth Rhurauf SRN, SCM, who had been the escort on 500 flights since her first mission with BEA in July 1965. In recognition of her work she was also awarded the Queen's Commendation for Valuable Service in the Air, becoming the first woman to receive this award. She accompanied her 1,000th patient on 12 July 1986. During 1979 Loganair had an Islander on 24-hour standby at Glasgow, and during the financial year 1978/9 transported 964 patients to sixty-five different hospitals in locations ranging from Shetland to London. By 1987 there were aircraft based at Kirkwall and Tingwall, as well as at the Glasgow base. This dealt mainly with calls from the Inner and Outer Hebrides and Kintyre. On one occasion Loganair had five planes airborne on air ambulance missions at the same time, and a sixth on stand-by duty.

In 1989 Bond Helicopters' Bolkow BO105D G-BATC was based at Dundee for an initial six-month trial period, with major sponsorship from British Telecom. The trial period was extended for a further six months, during which time the helicopter was transferred to Inverness Airport. In 1993 Bond Helicopters was awarded a contract to provide air ambulance cover with two Bolkow BO105Ds based at Inverness and Prestwick.

From 1993 Loganair Islander G-BPCA was painted in the livery of the Scottish Ambulance Service.

Another fatal accident befell an ambulance flight on 19 May 1996. Loganair Islander G-BEDZ had operated a mission to Inverness and was being ferried back to its base at Tingwall on Shetland when it made a missed approach in strong winds. On the second attempt the aircraft struck the ground at a steeply banked angle and the pilot was killed. The other two occupants survived.

During the winter of 1999–2000 the main runway at Glasgow Airport was closed from 2230hrs to 0540hrs each night for resurfacing. Loganair air ambulance flights used the northern taxiway for take-off and landing during these hours, and Islander G-BLNW was thus able to make the last revenue-earning airline departure of 1999 from Glasgow, departing at 2245hrs for Islay and landing back at 0015hrs on 1 January 2000, the first landing of the twenty-first century at Glasgow.

Just after midnight on 14–15 March 2005 Loganair lost another aircraft and crew on an air ambulance sortie. Islander G-BOMG had departed Glasgow for Campbeltown with a pilot and paramedic aboard. At the time of its arrival there was low cloud at around 400ft at Campbeltown, light winds and rain. During the approach the aircraft crashed into the sea off the Mull of Kintyre and both occupants were killed.

Gama Aviation had also been providing air ambulance aircraft at its Aberdeen Airport base, and on 26 January 2005 the company was awarded a contract for a seven-year period, commencing April 2006. The contract was valued at around £40 million and called for the provision of two Eurocopter EC-135 helicopters at Glasgow and Inverness, and two King Air 200C aircraft at Aberdeen and Glasgow. All the aircraft and helicopters were to be hired from Bond Air Services. They were equipped internally to the specifications of the Scottish Ambulance Service and were operated as part of the first fully-integrated, publicly-funded air ambulance service in the UK. In 2006 there were two EC-135 helicopters based at the Glasgow City Heliport and another at Inverness. From 2007 they were supported by a medically–equipped Super Puma search and rescue helicopter based in Shetland.

Loganair Islander G–BPCA in Scottish Air Ambulance livery at the RAF Leuchars Air Show in 1994. *(Author)*

Loganair Islander G–BEDZ was lost on Shetland whilst operating an air ambulance flight on 15 May 1996. *(Kieran Murray)*

Islander G-BLNW in Scottish Ambulance Service markings. *(Air-Britain)*

Bond Air Services King Air 200 G-SBAS landing at Aberdeen in 1997.

CHAPTER EIGHT

SCOTTISH AIRLINE PEOPLE

KATIE MACPHERSON

In 1936 Katie MacPherson joined her father, John, in the running of the landing strip on the beach at Barra. This was the beginning of a forty-five-year career that saw her working for five airlines in succession whilst still doing essentially the same job. The first services into Barra were operated by Northern and Scottish Airways, which was later merged with Highland Airways to form Scottish Airways. After the Second World War the independent airlines were nationalised and Miss MacPherson found herself working for British European Airways. On the retirement of her father the responsibility for the running of the airstrip passed to her brother Angus for a short period, but in 1951 she took charge as station manager. As part of her duties she could often be seen on the windswept beach, passing the latest weather and landing conditions to incoming flights via a hand-held radio. In 1969 she was awarded the MBE for her part in keeping Barra in touch with the rest of the world, and she was also to receive a Woman of the Year award. She transferred to British Airways when BEA merged with BOAC, and then moved to Loganair when that airline took over the Barra routes in 1975.

   In February 1980, not long after her retirement, Katie MacPherson suffered a stroke and had to be airlifted out in one of the air ambulance aircraft she had guided into Barra on so many occasions.

BEA Stornoway staff in the 1960s. From left to right: Sandy Murray (senior traffic officer), Bert Hayward (second officer), Alex MacRae (traffic assistant), Captain George Ebner, Robin Mackenzie (station superintendent). *(Robin Mackenzie)*

CAPTAIN DAVID BARCLAY MBE, O ST J.

David Barclay was the son of a Greenock dairyman and started taking flying lessons at Beardmore's Flying School. He was a founder member of the Scottish Flying Club in 1927 and set a new record by making his first solo flight after just 4 hours and 25 minutes of dual instruction. He joined the RAF in 1929 and served in India from 1930 to 1934. He then returned to Scotland where he joined Midland and Scottish Air Ferries, with whom he carried out the first of the many air ambulance flights that were a feature of his future career.

On 5 December 1934 he commanded the inaugural MSAF service from Renfrew to Skye in DH84 Dragon G-ACFG. In January the following year he inaugurated an extension of the route to South Uist, and in March 1936 he pioneered regular air services to North Uist. On 19 April 1940 he was transporting an Army general and his aides from Turnhouse to Orkney in DH84 G-ACNG, when the aircraft suddenly became nose-heavy on arrival at

Hatston Aerodrome and dived into the runway at a 45-degree angle. He sustained a smashed pelvis and ankle, broken ribs, a fractured nose and cuts and bruises and was hospitalised for 2½ months. The chances of him walking again, let alone flying, seemed slim, but after a few months he was back in the air, although the effects of his injuries did limit the types of aircraft he could fly. When BEA was formed after the war he transferred onto their Dakotas. He found that he could fly these well under normal conditions, but in emergency situations such as single-engined flight he could not apply the necessary extra force with his right foot. This problem effectively confined him to the smaller types such as the Rapide and the Heron.

Captain Barclay retired from BEA on 30 April 1965. His final flight was a scheduled Heron service from Barra and Tiree to Renfrew, which was delayed by the reception he received at both airfields, with the islanders turning out to see him off with farewell gifts.

During his career David Barclay had commanded around 3,000 of the 5,500 air ambulance flights made up till then, flying in all weather conditions. He had logged over 1.5 million miles and 18,000 flying hours, nearly all within Scotland. A plaque in his honour was erected on Islay and he flew there in a BEA Herald to unveil it. Captain David Barclay died in February 1981 at the age of seventy-five.

CAPTAIN ERIC STARLING FRMETS

Eric Starling gained his Aviator's Certificate at the age of nineteen, before he passed his driving test. He joined E.L. Gandar Dower as chief pilot of Aberdeen Airways on its inception in 1934, and was responsible for surveying routes for the airline from Aberdeen to Glasgow, Stromness and Shetland, and from Newcastle to Stavanger, flying the inaugural service on this route in a DH86B Express biplane on 12 July 1937. During the Second World War he served in RAF Coastal Command, and on the termination of hostilities he joined Scottish Airways at Inverness. Following the nationalisation of the internal air routes he joined BEA at Renfrew. On 1 April 1949 he flew a Dakota on BEA's inaugural service from Edinburgh to London. From 1949 until 1968 he was BEA's flight manager – Scotland, and was also heavily involved with the Air Ambulance Unit, for which he was a pilot from 1968 until his retirement in December 1971. At that time he was the most senior captain in BEA.

ROBERT MCKEAN OBE FCIT

Robert McKean began his aviation career as a Handley Page Hampden bomber pilot during the Second World War, and also served as an instructor on Tiger Moths. He was seconded from the RAF to BOAC and appointed staff manager – Africa. From a base in Durban he assisted in the setting up of the 'Horse Shoe Route' flying boat services around West Africa.

When BEA was set up in 1947 he was loaned by BOAC and was based at Ruislip as staff manager. In 1948 he moved to Renfrew, where he assumed responsibility for co-ordinating activities at the thirteen Scottish airports used by BEA, becoming BEA's first area manager for Scotland. He later became general manager and finally director of BEA's Scottish Division. When the BEA Scottish Airways Division was set up in 1971 he was appointed as its chairman. In 1966 he was awarded the OBE.

Robert McKean always had a particular interest in the air ambulance service, and assisted in its smooth handover from BEA to Loganair in 1973. He produced a short history of the service, and Loganair named Islander G-AXSS in his honour. He retired from BEA on 30 June 1973 after twenty-seven years' service.

CAPTAIN ALAN WHITFIELD

Alan Whitfield was born in Newcastle but moved to Canada to pursue a new life in farming. After a while he left the land and studied at the Alberta College of Technology before joining the Texas Gulf Corporation. Whilst with them he took up flying and subsequently became a commercial pilot. In 1962 he returned to the UK and joined Carlisle-based Cumberland Aviation. During his time there he was loaned to the Scottish Flying Club as an instructor and this led to his introduction to Captain McIntosh of Loganair. After a period with Strathallan Air Services Captain Whitfield finally joined Loganair, becoming their first pilot without an RAF or Royal Navy flying background.

He was sent to Shetland to develop local air services and was responsible for the construction of airstrips on many of the outer islands, including Foula, Papa Stour and the Outer Skerries, as well as the development of Tingwall airfield as a more convenient airfield for Lerwick than Sumburgh. In 1978 Captain Whitfield left Shetland to become Loganair's chief training captain, based at Glasgow. In 1979 he was awarded the Queen's Commendation for Valuable Service in the Air, in recognition of his role in developing inter-island travel in Shetland and his completion of over 400 air ambulance missions. He left Loganair on 30 December 1981 to return to his first love – the land. He went on to provide ranger services in Kintail on behalf of the National Trust for Scotland, before retiring to the north-east of Scotland.

SCOTTISH AIRLINES' PROPOSED WORLDWIDE ROUTE NETWORK, 1946

Air Services by Scottish Aviation

Proposed Schedules on Internal, European, and Trans-Atlantic Routes

THIS PROPOSED SCHEDULE of airline operations is issued in advance in order that business men and those returning from abroad may have some information of the services which are likely to be available to the United Kingdom in general and the Northern industrial area in particular.

There are many kinds of commercial air transport. The only kind good enough for Britain is that which supports itself by the enlargement of travel and trade.

The pattern of airline expansion which Scottish Aviation proposes has one basic principle. That is to provide the greatest possible variety of service at the lowest possible rates for passengers and freight.

The Prestwick organisation offers intensive *economic* development of air service, utilising a relatively small number of ultra-efficient commercial aircraft until equipment can be produced in Britain for the movement of air traffic in volume at rates equivalent to third class surface fares.

It wants no subsidy. It wants neither monopoly nor quasi-judicial "protection" and hopes, indeed, that it will have regulated competition from other British companies on every route.

No single organisation, no one group of established companies, is big enough to handle post-war air commerce on behalf of the 50 million people of the United Kingdom.

And Scottish Aviation is an aviation company, concerned first, last, and all the time, with the orderly development of British aviation.

What it offers right now is, in fact, the greatest possible variety of airline service at the lowest possible rates for the area which it has been serving in other ways through the past ten years.

The Prestwick organisation is the only one in Britain ready, willing, and able, to start immediately to supplement the war-time air services of the United Kingdom with genuine commercial services.

It possesses all of the aviation leadership, the technical skill, and practical experience of long-distance and short-distance air transport that are required to operate an integrated unit of airlines on a modern scale.

The service which it will provide will be complete service for the passenger. The standards of comfort and convenience which have been set for passengers are standards set by aviation men.

As war-time restrictions are removed you will discover in flying with Scottish Aviation that the world has become a smaller place; that the Scottish air liner is indeed a magic carpet on which every wish is anticipated, and by which you can skip from continent to continent during a holiday week-end, or on a three or four days business trip.

The fares shown in these schedules may be subject to slight modifications. There is still a number of unknown factors which hinders the calculation of the cost of point-to-point mileages. Landing rights, taxation on fuel, and the cost of local services are matters which must await settlement pending International negotiations.

Travel between Prestwick and certain foreign centres may cost you slightly less; travel between Prestwick and one or two others may cost you a little more.

In certain instances the indicated choice of British airports is provisional, and will be finally determined according to demand.

But Scottish Aviation offers a fare of approximately 2¼d a mile on nearly every route, subject to fractional modifications if circumstances should make them necessary.

2

All fares include the cost of full insurance of passengers and baggage, and of the incidental services on every flight.

All meals will be served free on board at normal meal hours. Tipping will be forbidden.

From the moment you lift your telephone or call at the airport ticket office to book a passage until you arrive at your destination you will be an honoured guest of the airline.

In the event of interruption of services on any route, all alternative means of forward travel will be arranged and paid for, on your behalf, by the airline and refunds made, if applicable.

Ground transport will be arranged to give centre to centre service between all cities.

Negotiations are proceeding to make a "drive yourself" car hire service available at every port of call for the convenience of passengers.

It will be easy to get around the world by Scottish Aviation, and it will not be costly.

In order that you may plan your trips more easily, the airline will issue only single tickets. Thus you may go by air and come back, if you wish, by land or sea, or rejoin the Scottish airline at any point on any route.

The job of reconstruction which Britain has to do will be done the quicker with the aid of Scottish Aviation. To restore British economy, to enlarge the channels of trade, to speed the establishment and renewal of business contacts is a process to which this Scottish airline system can make a tremendous *practical* contribution.

There never was a period in history when the immediate future was so full of opportunity for new enterprise and new methods of trade and commerce.

We are on the threshold of a second Industrial Revolution occasioned by a new, fast and flexible medium of world transport, with three-quarters of the world's territory awaiting development.

And when the time comes for the restoration of peace-time holidays and holiday travel, look to Scottish Aviation to give you a new diversity of pleasures and excursions in sunny lands.

The aeroplane is a practical, swift vehicle which brings all of the globe within your compass.

3

SERVICE ON THE NORTH ATLANTIC

Night and Day Schedules to Canada and the U.S. give you choice of route and.choice of rates

PRESTWICK TO NEW YORK—
NIGHT SLEEPER SERVICE

Fare: £47 Single.
„ £94 Return.

Stage Fares	Miles			
£30 10 0	2090	PRESTWICK	.............dep.	8.30 p.m.
		GANDER	.............arr.	7.30 a.m.
£16 10 0	1114	GANDER	.............dep.	8.30 a.m.
		NEW YORK	.............arr.	2.00 p.m.
				(9 a.m. N.Y. time).
£16 10 0	1114	NEW YORK	.............dep.	6.30 p.m.
			(1.30 p.m. N.Y. time).	
		GANDER	.............arr.	11.20 p.m.
£30 10 0	2090	GANDER	.............dep.	12.20 a.m.
		PRESTWICK	.............arr.	10.00 a.m.

4

The Scottish Airlines proposed worldwide route system.

PRESTWICK TO NEW YORK—

DAY SERVICE

Fare: £40 Single.
„ £80 Return.

Stage Fares	Miles			
£9 8 0	844	PRESTWICK	.............dep.	7.00 a.m.
		ICELAND	.............arr.	11.30 a.m.
£9 17 0	885	ICELAND	.............dep.	12.30 p.m.
		B'WEST	.............arr.	5.30 p.m.
£7 17 0	708	B'WEST	.............dep.	6.30 p.m.
		GOOSE BAY	.............arr.	10.15 p.m.
£9 0 0	809	GOOSE BAY	.............dep.	11.15 p.m.
		MONTREAL	.............arr.	3.30 a.m.
£3 18 0	369	MONTREAL	.............dep.	4.30 a.m.
		NEW YORK	.............arr.	6.30 a.m.
				(1.30 a.m. N.Y. time).
£3 18 0	369	NEW YORK	.............dep.	2.30 a.m.
			(9.30 p.m. N.Y. time).	
		MONTREAL	.............arr.	4.30 a.m.
£9 0 0	809	MONTREAL	.............dep.	5.30 a.m.
		GOOSE BAY	.............arr.	9.45 a.m.
£7 17 0	708	GOOSE BAY	.............dep.	10.45 a.m.
		B'WEST	.............arr.	2.30 p.m.
£9 17 0	885	B'WEST	.............dep.	3.30 p.m.
		ICELAND	.............arr.	8.30 p.m.
£9 8 0	844	ICELAND	.............dep.	9.30 p.m.
		PRESTWICK	.............arr.	2.00 a.m.

5

SERVICE FOR THE
UNITED KINGDOM

The Shuttle Schedules :
door-to-door transit for
trans-Atlantic and local
passengers saves time

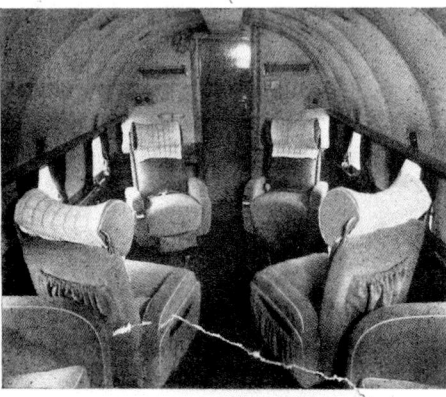

In certain instances, the indicated choice of British airports is provisional, and will be finally determined according to demand. In all instances, ground transport will be arranged to give centre to centre service between all cities. All fares include the cost of full insurance of passengers and baggage. All meals will be served free on board at normal meal hours. Tipping will be forbidden. From the moment you lift your telephone or call at the airport ticket office to book a place until you arrive at your destination you will be an honoured guest of the airline.

6

PRESTWICK TO HEATHROW
(GLASGOW)   (LONDON)
(via BURTONWOOD)
Fare: £3 9s 6d Single.
„ £6 19s 0d Return.

Stage Fares	Miles							
£1 14 6	166	PRESTWICK .... dep. (Glasgow)	8.00 a.m.	10.40 a.m.	1.30 p.m.	4.40 p.m.	7.30 p.m.	
		BURTONWOOD .... arr. (Liverpool & Manchester).		11.48 a.m. Direct	2.38 p.m.	5.48 p.m.		Direct
		BURTONWOOD .... dep. (Liverpool & Manchester).		11.53 a.m.	2.43 p.m.	5.53 p.m.		
£1 15 0	168	HEATHROW .... arr. (London).	10.10 a.m.	1.02 p.m.	3.52 p.m.	7.02 p.m.	9.40 p.m.	
£1 15 0	168	HEATHROW .... dep. (London).	8.00 a.m.	10.30 a.m.	1.40 p.m.	4.30 p.m.	7.30 p.m.	
		BURTONWOOD .... arr. (Liverpool & Manchester).		11.39 a.m. Direct	2.49 p.m.	5.39 p.m.		Direct
		BURTONWOOD .... dep. (Liverpool & Manchester).		11.44 a.m.	2.54 p.m.	5.44 p.m.		
£1 14 6	166	PRESTWICK .... arr. (Glasgow).	10.10 a.m.	12.52 p.m.	4.02 p.m.	6.52 p.m.	9.40 p.m.	

7

GRANGEMOUTH OR EDINBURGH TO LONDON
(via NEWCASTLE & DONCASTER)

Fare: £3 13s Single.
„ £7 6s Return.

Stage Fares	Miles						
		GRANGEMOUTH					
£0 19 0	90	or EDINBURGH............dep.	7.50 a.m.	10.30 a.m.	1.45 p.m.	5.10 p.m.	8.10 p.m.
		NEWCASTLE ....arr.	11.11 a.m.	2.26 p.m.	5.51 p.m.		
£1 3 0	109	NEWCASTLE ....dep.	11.16 a.m.	2.31 p.m.	5.56 p.m.		
		DONCASTER ....arr. Direct	12.4 p.m.	3.19 p.m.	6.44 p.m.	Direct	
£1 11 0	148	DONCASTER ....dep.	12.9 p.m.	3.24 p.m.	6.49 p.m.		
		LONDON ....arr.	10.00 a.m.	1.11 p.m.	4.26 p.m.	7.51 p.m.	10.20 p.m.

Stage Fares	Miles					
£1 11 0	148	LONDON ....dep.	7.50 a.m.	10.30 a.m.	1.45 p.m.	8.10 p.m.
		DONCASTER ....arr.	11.32 a.m.	2.47 p.m.		
£1 3 0	109	DONCASTER ....dep.	11.37 a.m.	2.52 p.m.		
		NEWCASTLE ....arr. Direct	12.25 p.m.	3.40 p.m.	Direct	
£0 19 0	90	NEWCASTLE ....dep.	12.30 p.m.	3.45 p.m.		
		EDINBURGH or				
		GRANGEMOUTH ....arr.	10.00 a.m.	1.11 p.m.	4.26 p.m.	10.20 p.m.

RENFREW TO HEATHROW
(Glasgow)   (London)

Fare: £3 11 6d Single.
„ £7 3s 0 Return.

Miles		Miles	
	RENFREW ......dep. 9.00 a.m.		HEATHROW ....dep. 6.30 p.m.
343	(Glasgow).	343	(London).
	HEATHROW ....arr. 11.46 a.m.		RENFREW ......arr. 8.46 p.m.
	(London).		(Glasgow).

LONDON TO PARIS.

Fare: £2 5s Single.
„ £4 10s Return.

Miles	
215	LONDON ....dep. 10.40 a.m. 2.30 p.m. 6.20 p.m.
	PARIS ....arr. 12.5 p.m. 3.55 p.m. 7.45 p.m.
215	PARIS ....dep. 8.45 a.m. 12.35 p.m. 4.25 p.m.
	LONDON ....arr. 10.10 a.m. 2.00 p.m. 5.50 p.m.

PRESTWICK TO BRISTOL
(via BURTONWOOD)

Fare: £3 4s Single.
„ £6 8s Return.

Stage Fares	Miles			
£1 14 6	165	PRESTWICK ....dep.	9.00 a.m.	2.30 p.m.
		BURTONWOOD..arr.	10.08 a.m.	3.38 p.m.
		(Liverpool, Manchester).		
£1 9 6	142	BURTONWOOD..dep.	10.13 a.m.	3.43 p.m.
		(Liverpool, Manchester).		
		BRISTOL ....arr.	11.13 a.m.	4.43 p.m.
£1 9 6	142	BRISTOL ....dep.	11.45 a.m.	5.20 p.m.
		BURTONWOOD. arr.	12.45 p.m.	6.20 p.m.
		(Liverpool, Manchester).		
£1 14 6	165	BURTONWOOD..dep.	12.50 p.m.	6.25 p.m.
		(Liverpool, Manchester).		
		PRESTWICK .....arr.	1.58 p.m.	7.33 p.m.

DUBLIN TO DONCASTER
(via BURTONWOOD)

Fare: £2 6s Single.
„ £4 12s Return.

Stage Fares	Miles			
£1 12 0	154	DUBLIN ....dep.	10.45 a.m.	3.10 p.m.
		BURTONWOOD ..arr.	11.48 a.m.	4.14 p.m.
		(Liverpool, Manchester).		
£0 14 0	67	BURTONWOOD..dep.	11.53 a.m.	4.19 p.m.
		(Liverpool, Manchester).		
		DONCASTER ....arr.	12.26 p.m.	4.51 p.m.
£0 14 0	67	DONCASTER ....dep.	12.40 p.m.	5.10 p.m.
		BURTONWOOD ..arr.	1.12 p.m.	5.42 p.m.
		(Liverpool, Manchester).		
£1 12 0	154	BURTONWOOD..dep.	1.17 p.m.	5.47 p.m.
		(Liverpool, Manchester).		
		DUBLIN ....arr.	2.21 p.m.	6.49 p.m.

DUBLIN TO ABERDEEN
(via PRESTWICK & GRANGEMOUTH)

Fare: £3 9s Single.
„ £6 18s Return.

Stage Fares	Miles			
£1 0 0	96	DUBLIN ....dep.	8.42 a.m.	1.42 p.m.
		BELFAST ....arr.	9.25 a.m.	2.25 p.m.
£0 17 0	80	BELFAST ....dep.	9.30 a.m.	2.30 p.m.
		PRESTWICK ....arr.	10.07 a.m.	3.07 p.m.
£0 10 0	48	PRESTWICK ....dep.	10.12 a.m.	3.12 p.m.
		GRANGEMOUTH arr.	10.37 a.m.	3.37 p.m.
£0 7 6	35	GRANGEMOUTH dep.	10.42 a.m.	3.42 p.m.
		ERROL ....arr.	11.03 a.m.	4.03 p.m.
		(Perth, Dundee).		
£0 14 6	68	ERROL ....dep.	11.08 a.m.	4.08 p.m.
		(Perth, Dundee).		
		ABERDEEN ......arr.	11.41 a.m.	4.41 p.m.
£0 14 6	68	ABERDEEN .....dep.	6.11 p.m.	11.39 a.m.
		ERROL ....arr.	6.44 p.m.	12.12 p.m.
		(Perth, Dundee).		
£0 7 6	35	ERROL ....dep.	6.49 p.m.	12.17 p.m.
		(Perth, Dundee).		
		GRANGEMOUTH arr.	7.10 p.m.	12.38 p.m.
£0 10 0	48	GRANGEMOUTH dep.	7.15 p.m.	12.43 p.m.
		PRESTWICK ....arr.	7.40 p.m.	1.08 p.m.
£0 17 0	80	PRESTWICK ....dep.	7.45 p.m.	1.13 p.m.
		BELFAST ....arr.	8.22 p.m.	1.50 p.m.
£1 0 0	96	BELFAST ....dep.	8.27 p.m.	1.55 p.m.
		DUBLIN ....arr.	9.10 p.m.	2.38 p.m.

DAY SERVICE FOR
WESTERN EUROPE

An integrated travel system for the nearer Continental countries

PRESTWICK TO STOCKHOLM
(via ABERDEEN & OSLO)
DAILY SERVICE

Fare: £9 10s Single.
" £19 Return.

Stage Fares	Miles			
£1 11 6	151	PRESTWICK	....dep. 10.30 a.m.	4.30 p.m.
		ABERDEEN	......arr. 11.33 a.m.	5.33 p.m.
£5 4 0	498	ABERDEEN	......dep. 11.43 a.m.	5.43 p.m.
		OSLO	............arr. 2.52 p.m.	8.52 p.m.
£2 14 6	260	OSLO	............dep. 3.02 p.m.	9.02 p.m.
		STOCKHOLM	....arr. 4.44 p.m.	10.44 p.m.
£2 14 6	260	STOCKHOLM	....dep. 9.30 a.m.	5.30 p.m.
		OSLO	......arr. 11.12 a.m.	7.12 p.m.
£5 4 0	498	OSLO	............dep. 11.22 a.m.	7.22 p.m.
		ABERDEEN	......arr. 2.31 p.m.	10.31 p.m.
£1 11 6	151	ABERDEEN	......dep. 2.41 p.m.	10.41 p.m.
		PRESTWICK	......arr. 3.44 p.m.	11.44 p.m.

14

PRESTWICK TO AMSTERDAM
(via CARLISLE & DONCASTER)
DAILY SERVICE

Fare: £4 17s Single
" £9 14s Return

Stage Fares	Miles			
£0 16 0	75	PRESTWICK	....dep. 11.00 a.m.	2.00 p.m.
		CARLISLE	......arr. 11.35 a.m.	2.35 p.m.
£1 6 6	127	CARLISLE	......dep. 11.40 a.m.	2.40 p.m.
		DONCASTER	...arr. 12.34 p.m.	3.34 p.m.
£2 14 6	260	DONCASTER	...dep. 12.39 p.m.	3.39 p.m.
		AMSTERDAM	...arr. 2.21 p.m.	5.21 p.m.
£2 14 6	260	AMSTERDAM	...dep. 10.00 a.m.	3.50 p.m.
		DONCASTER	....arr. 11.42 a.m.	4.42 p.m.
£1 6 6	127	DONCASTER	....dep. 11.47 a.m.	4.47 p.m.
		CARLISLE	......arr. 12.41 p.m.	5.41 p.m.
£0 16 0	75	CARLISLE	......dep. 12.46 p.m.	5.46 p.m.
		PRESTWICK	......arr. 1.21 p.m.	6.21 p.m.

PRESTWICK TO HAMBURG
(via NEWCASTLE)
DAILY SERVICE

Fare: £6 5s Single.
" £12 10s Return

Stage Fares	Miles			
£1 5 0	120	PRESTWICK	...dep. 10.20 a.m.	3.00 p.m.
		NEWCASTLE	...arr. 11.12 a.m.	3.52 p.m.
£5 0 0	480	NEWCASTLE	....dep. 11.22 a.m.	4.02 p.m.
		HAMBURG	......arr. 2.25 p.m.	7.05 p.m.
£5 0 0	480	HAMBURG	......dep. 10.00 a.m.	2.45 p.m.
		NEWCASTLE	...arr. 1.03 p.m.	5.48 p.m.
£1 5 0	120	NEWCASTLE	...dep. 1.13 p.m.	5.58 p.m.
		PRESTWICK	...arr. 2.05 p.m.	6.50 p.m.

15

SERVICE FOR THE FAR EAST, via MOSCOW

Fare: £59 17s 6d Single
" £119 15s Return.

Stage Fare	Miles		
£6 17 6	661	PRESTWICK	........dep. 10.00 a.m. Mon.
£10 2 6	972	COPENHAGEN	......arr. 1.37 p.m. "
			dep. 2.37 p.m. "
£14 15 6	1419	MOSCOW	............arr. 7.52 p.m. "
			dep. 8.52 p.m. "
£13 2 6	1260	OMSK	................arr. 4.28 a.m. Tues.
			dep. 5.28 a.m. "
£14 19 6	1438	IRKUTSK	...........arr. 12.14 p.m. "
			dep. 1.14 p.m. "
		VLADIVOSTOK	.....arr. 8.56 p.m. "
£14 19 6	1438	VLADIVOSTOK	.....dep. 9.00 a.m. Mon.
		IRKUTSK	...........arr. 4.42 p.m. "
£13 2 6	1260		dep. 5.42 p.m. "
		OMSK	................arr. 12.28 a.m. Tues.
£14 15 6	1419		dep. 1.28 a.m. "
		MOSCOW	............arr. 9.04 a.m. "
£10 2 6	972		dep. 10.04 a.m. "
		COPENHAGEN	......arr. 3.19 p.m. "
£6 17 6	661		dep. 4.19 p.m. "
		PRESTWICK	........arr. 7.55 p.m. "

SERVICE FOR THE FAR EAST, via the MEDITERRANEAN and INDIA

Fare: £111 10s Single.
" £223 Return.

Stage Fares	Miles		
£3 9 0	332	PRESTWICK	...... dep. 9.00 a.m. Mon.
£2 5 0	215	LONDON	...........arr. 11.09 a.m. "
			dep. 11.24 a.m. "
		PARIS	............arr. 12.50 p.m. "

16

Stage Fares	Miles		
£4 5 6	410	PARIS	............dep. 1.35 p.m. Mon.
£3 18 0	374	MARSEILLES	........arr. 4.12 p.m. "
			dep. 4.42 p.m. "
£6 15 0	648	ROME	...............arr. 7.06 p.m. "
			dep. 7.51 p.m. "
£7 7 0	707	ATHENS	............arr. 11.55 p.m. "
			dep. 12.40 a.m. Tues.
£2 17 0	274	CAIRO	...............arr. 5.05 a.m. "
			dep. 5.40 a.m. "
£5 14 0	548	JERUSALEM	........arr. 7.28 a.m. "
			dep. 7.48 a.m. "
£2 19 0	282	BAGHDAD	........arr. 11.15 a.m. "
			dep. 12.00 noon "
£2 6 0	220	BASRA	...............arr. 1.51 p.m. "
			dep. 2.06 p.m. "
£3 15 0	360	BUSHIRE	...........arr. 3.34 p.m. "
			dep. 3.49 p.m. "
£7 7 0	706	BANDAR ABBAS	....arr. 6.08 p.m. "
			dep. 6.43 p.m. "
£6 15 6	651	KARACHI	...........arr. 11.08 p.m. "
			dep. 11.53 p.m. "
£8 10 0	817	DELHI	...............arr. 3.58 a.m. Wed.
			dep. 4.28 a.m. "
£6 15 0	649	CALCUTTA	.........arr. 9.33 a.m. "
			dep. 10.03 a.m. "
£7 5 6	699	RANGOON	........arr. 2.07 p.m. "
			dep. 2.37 p.m. "
£5 13 6	544	HANOI	...............arr. 6.59 p.m. "
			dep. 7.44 p.m. "
£8 0 6	771	HONG KONG	......arr. 11.11 p.m. "
			dep. 11.41 p.m. "
£6 18 6	664	SHANGHAI	........arr. 4.29 a.m. Thur.
			dep. 4.59 a.m. "
£8 14 0	835	PEKING	............arr. 9.08 a.m. "
			dep. 9.38 a.m. "
		VLADIVOSTOK	....arr. 2.50 p.m. "

17

SERVICE FROM THE MIDDLE EAST, via INDIA and the MEDITERRANEAN

Stage Fares	Miles			
		VLADIVOSTOK	....dep.	9.00 a.m. Mon.
£8 14 0	835			
		PEKING	..........arr.	2.12 p.m. ,,
£6 18 6	664		dep.	2.42 p.m. ,,
		SHANGHAI	..........arr.	6.51 p.m. ,,
£8 0 6	771		dep.	7.21 p.m. ,,
		HONG KONG	........arr.	12.09 a.m. Tues.
£5 13 6	544		dep.	12.39 a.m. ,,
		HANOI	..............arr.	4.05 a.m. ,,
£7 5 6	699		dep.	4.50 a.m. ,,
		RANGOON	..........arr.	9.12 a.m. ,,
£6 15 0	649		dep.	9.42 a.m. ,,
		CALCUTTA	........arr.	1.46 p.m. ,,
£8 10 0	817		dep.	2.16 p.m. ,,
		DELHI	..............arr.	7.21 p.m. ,,
£6 15 6	651		dep.	7.51 p.m. ,,
		KARACHI	..........arr.	11.56 p.m. ,,
£7 7 0	706		dep.	12.41 a.m. Wed.
		BANDAR ABBAS	....arr.	5.06 a.m. ,,
£3 15 0	360		dep.	5.41 a.m. ,,
		BUSHIRE	..........arr.	8.00 a.m. ,,
£2 6 0	220		dep.	8.15 a.m. ,,
		BASRA	..............arr.	9.43 a.m. ,,
£2 19 0	282		dep.	9.58 a.m. ,,
		BAGHDAD	..........arr.	11.49 a.m. ,,
£5 14 0	548		dep.	12.34 p.m. ,,
		JERUSALEM	........arr.	4.01 p.m. ,,
£2 17 0	274		dep.	4.21 p.m. ,,
		CAIRO	..............arr.	6.09 p.m. ,,
£7 7 0	707		dep.	6.44 p.m. ,,
		ATHENS	..........arr.	11.09 p.m. ,,
£6 15 0	648		dep.	11.54 p.m. ,,
		ROME	..............arr.	3.58 a.m. Thur.

18

Stage Fares	Miles			
		ROME	..............dep.	4.43 a.m. Thur.
£3 18 0	374			
		MARSEILLES	........arr.	7.07 a.m. ,,
£4 5 6	410		dep.	7.37 a.m. ,,
		PARIS	..............arr.	10.14 a.m. ,,
£2 5 0	215		dep.	10.59 a.m. ,,
		LONDON	..........arr.	12.25 p.m. ,,
£3 9 0	332		dep.	12.40 p.m. ,,
		PRESTWICK	........arr.	2.50 p.m. ,,

EXPRESS SERVICE FOR INDIA— PRESTWICK TO KARACHI

Fare: £45 18s Single.
,, £91 16s Return.

Stage Fares	Miles			
		PRESTWICK	........dep.	9.30 a.m. Mon.
£9 2 0	874			
		PRAGUE	..............arr.	2.14 p.m. ,,
£9 19 0	954		dep.	3.14 p.m. ,,
		ISTAMBUL	..........arr.	8.23 p.m. ,,
£13 9 0	1290		dep.	9.23 p.m. ,,
		BASRA	..............arr.	4.18 a.m. Tues.
£13 8 0	1286		dep.	5.18 a.m. ,,
		KARACHI	..........arr.	12.12 p.m. ,,
		KARACHI	..........dep.	9.00 a.m. Mon.
£13 8 0	1286			
		BASRA	..............arr.	3.54 p.m. ,,
£13 9 0	1290		dep.	4.54 p.m. ,,
		ISTAMBUL	..........arr.	11.49 p.m. ,,
£9 19 0	954		dep.	12.49 a.m. Tues.
		PRAGUE	..............arr.	5.58 a.m. ,,
£9 2 0	874		dep.	6.58 a.m. ,,
		PRESTWICK	........arr.	11.42 a.m. ,,

19

SERVICE FOR THE MIDDLE EAST, via CENTRAL EUROPE— PRESTWICK TO BAGHDAD

Fare: £30 2s 6d Single.
,, £60 5s Return.

Stage Fares	Miles			
		PRESTWICK	........dep.	8.30 a.m. Mon.
£4 10 6	435			
		AMSTERDAM	......arr.	11.16 a.m. ,,
£2 7 0	225		dep.	12.01 p.m. ,,
		FRANKFURT	......arr.	1.31 p.m. ,,
£3 17 6	371		dep.	2.01 p.m. ,,
		VIENNA	............arr.	4.24 p.m. ,,
£1 7 6	133		dep.	4.54 p.m. ,,
		BUDAPEST	..........arr.	5.50 p.m. ,,
£2 2 0	202		dep.	6.35 p.m. ,,
		BELGRADE	........arr.	7.56 p.m. ,,
£2 2 6	204		dep.	8.26 p.m. ,,
		SOFIA	..............arr.	9.48 p.m. ,,
£3 5 0	312		dep.	10.33 p.m. ,,
		ISTAMBUL	..........arr.	12.34 a.m. Tues.
£5 15 6	555		dep.	1.04 a.m. ,,
		ALEPPO	..........arr.	4.34 a.m. ,,
£4 15 0	457		dep.	5.19 a.m. ,,
		BAGHDAD	..........arr.	8.13 a.m. ,,
		BAGHDAD	........dep.	9.00 a.m. Mon.
£4 15 0	457			
		ALEPPO	..............arr.	11.54 a.m. ,,
£5 15 6	555		dep.	12.39 p.m. ,,
		ISTAMBUL	..........arr.	4.09 p.m. ,,
£3 5 0	312		dep.	4.39 p.m. ,,
		SOFIA	..............arr.	6.40 p.m. ,,
£2 2 6	204		dep.	7.25 p.m. ,,
		BELGRADE	........arr.	8.47 p.m. ,,
£2 2 0	202		dep.	9.17 p.m. ,,
		BUDAPEST	..........arr.	10.38 p.m. ,,
£1 7 6	133		dep.	11.23 p.m. ,,
		VIENNA	..............arr.	12.19 a.m. Tues.
£3 17 6	371		dep.	12.49 a.m. ,,
		FRANKFURT	......arr.	3.12 a.m. ,,
£2 7 0	225		dep.	3.42 a.m. ,,
		AMSTERDAM	......arr.	5.12 a.m. ,,
£4 10 6	435		dep.	5.57 a.m. ,,
		PRESTWICK	........arr.	8.43 a.m. ,,

SCOTTISH ROUTES OPERATED BY BEA

From Aberdeen to:

Inverness	1 November 1968–31 October 1970
Jersey (via Edinburgh)	9 June 1957–30 September 1960
Kirkwall (some via Wick)	1 February 1947–BA merger
Sumburgh (some via Wick and Kirkwall	1 February 1947–BA merger
Wick	1 February 1947–BA merger

From Edinburgh to:

Aberdeen	1 February 1947–BA merger
Inverness	1 April 1967–30 September 1969
Jersey	9 June 1957–BA merger
Kirkwall (via Aberdeen and Wick)	1 February 1947–BA merger
Sumburgh (via Aberdeen or via Aberdeen, Wick and Kirkwall)	1 February 1947–BA merger
Wick (via Aberdeen)	1 February 1947–BA merger

From Glasgow to:

Aberdeen (some via Edinburgh)	1 February 1947–BA merger
Barra (some via Tiree)	1 February 1947–BA merger
Belfast	1 February 1947–BA merger
Benbecula (some via Tiree)	1 February 1947–BA merger

Campbeltown	1 February 1947–BA merger
Copenhagen	11 August 1947–1 December 1947
Edinburgh	1 February 1947–BA merger
Guernsey	4 June 1955–BA merger
Islay (some via Campbeltown)	1 February 1947–BA merger
Isle of Man	21 April 1947–31 October 1954 (suspended between October 1948 and 1 April 1951)
Jersey (some via Guernsey)	1 April 1951–BA merger (suspended between 30 September 1952 and 1 June 1955)
Kirkwall (via Inverness and Wick or via Edinburgh, Aberdeen and Wick)	1 February 1947–BA merger
Malta (via Birmingham)	1 April 1969–27 October 1973
Palma (some via Manchester)	1 April 1964–25 October 1970
Paris (via Manchester or Birmingham)	28 April 1950–BA merger
Perth	1 July 1950–31 August 1950
Stornoway	1 February 1947–BA merger
Sumburgh (via Inverness, Wick and Kirkwall or via Aberdeen, Wick and Kirkwall)	1 February 1947–BA merger
Tiree (some via Islay)	1 February 1947–BA merger
Wick (via Inverness or via Edinburgh and Aberdeen)	1 February 1947–BA merger

From Inverness to:

Benbecula (some via Stornoway)	1 February 1947–BA merger
Kirkwall (some via Wick)	1 February 1947–BA merger
Stornoway	1 February 1947–BA merger
Sumburgh (via Wick and Kirkwall)	1 February 1947–BA merger
Wick	1 February 1947–BA merger

From Kirkwall to:

Sumburgh	1 February 1947–BA merger (services operated from Hatston until 1950, then from Grimsetter)

From Prestwick to:

Belfast	1 February 1947–6 October 1947
Glasgow	1 February 1947–6 October 1947

From Stornoway to:

Barra (via Benbecula)	1 February 1947–30 September 1952
Benbecula	1 February 1947–BA merger

All-cargo services from Glasgow to:

Amsterdam (via Manchester)	1 November 1970–BA merger
Frankfurt (via Manchester and London)	1 November 1970–BA merger

ROUTE MAPS SHOWING THE DEVELOPMENT OF LOGANAIR NETWORK

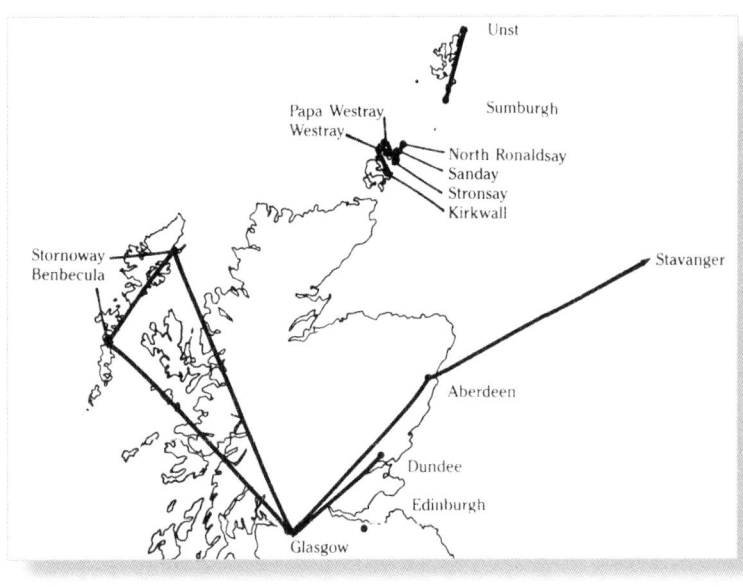

1970. Reproduced from *The Story of Loganair*, by Iain Hutchison, and used by kind permission of Iain Hutchison.

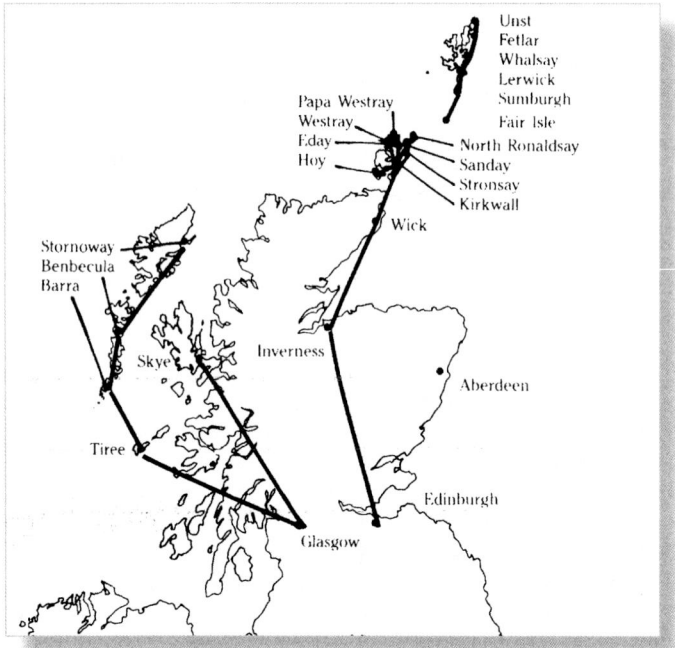

1976. Reproduced from *The Story of Loganair*, by Iain Hutchison, and used by kind permission of Iain Hutchison.

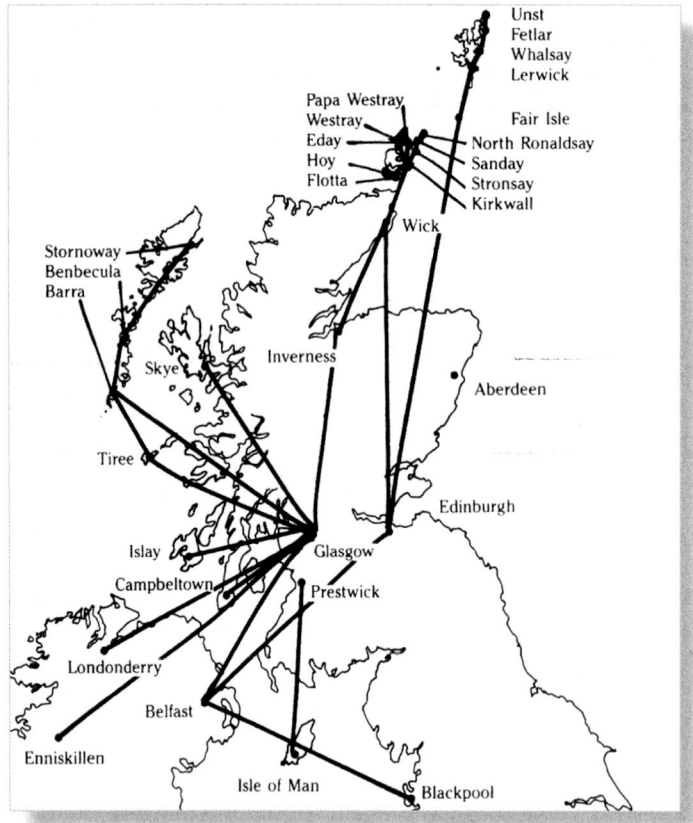

1981. Reproduced from *The Story of Loganair*, by Iain Hutchison, and used by kind permission of Iain Hutchison.

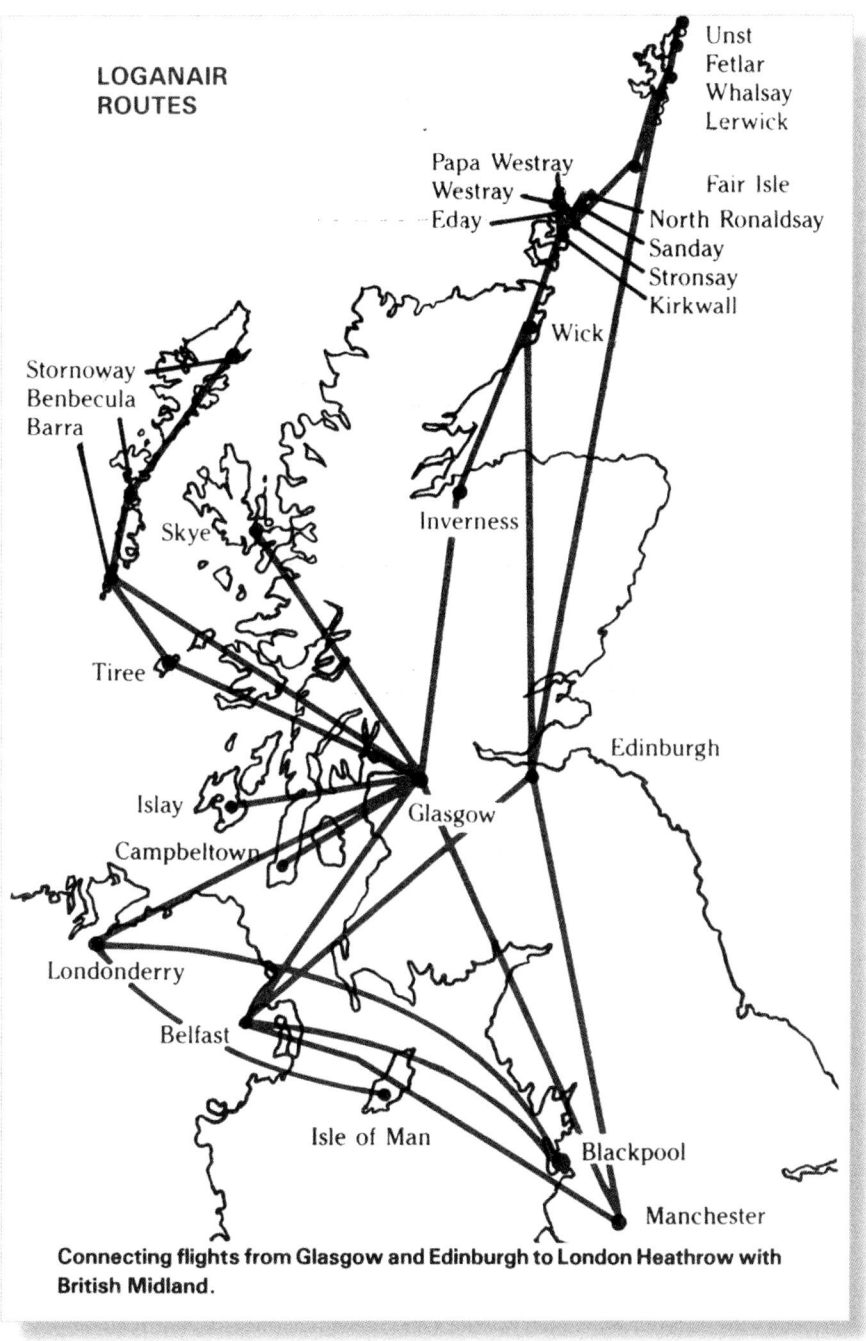

**LOGANAIR
ROUTES**

Unst
Fetlar
Whalsay
Lerwick

Papa Westray
Westray
Eday

Fair Isle
North Ronaldsay
Sanday
Stronsay
Kirkwall

Wick

Stornoway
Benbecula
Barra

Skye

Inverness

Tiree

Edinburgh

Islay

Glasgow

Campbeltown

Londonderry

Belfast

Isle of Man

Blackpool

Manchester

**Connecting flights from Glasgow and Edinburgh to London Heathrow with
British Midland.**

1987.

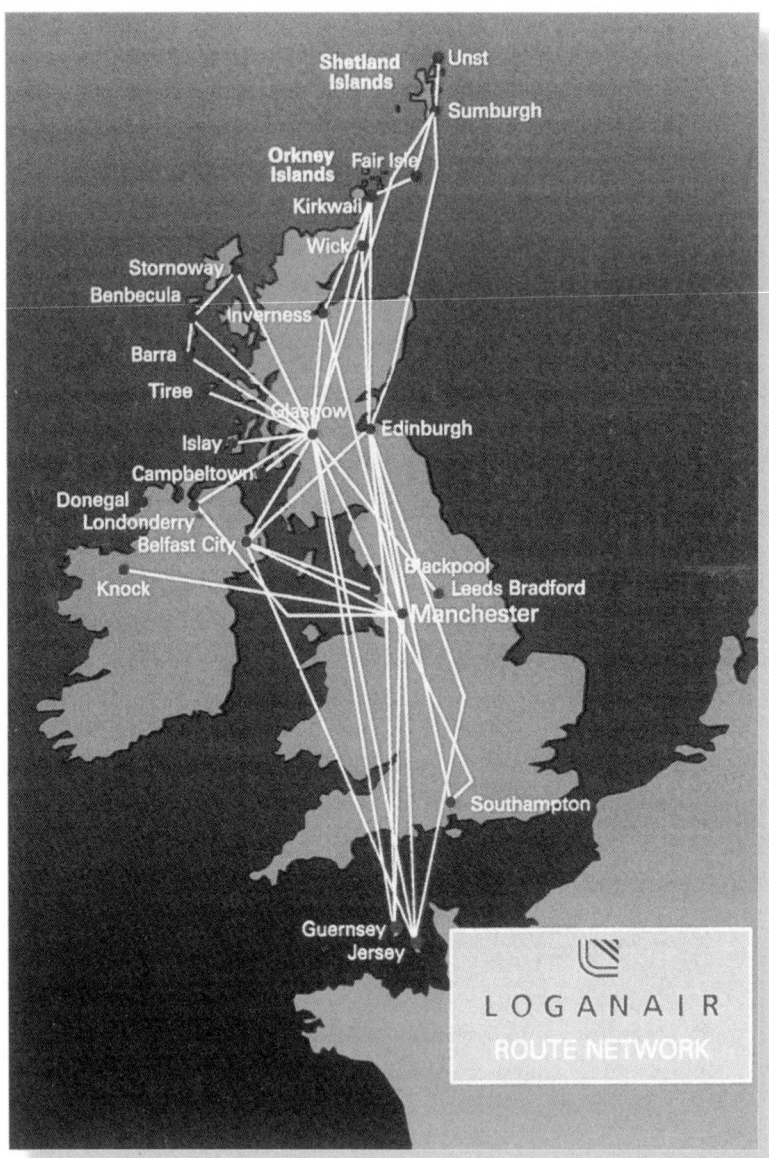

1992.

TICKETS AND ROUTES

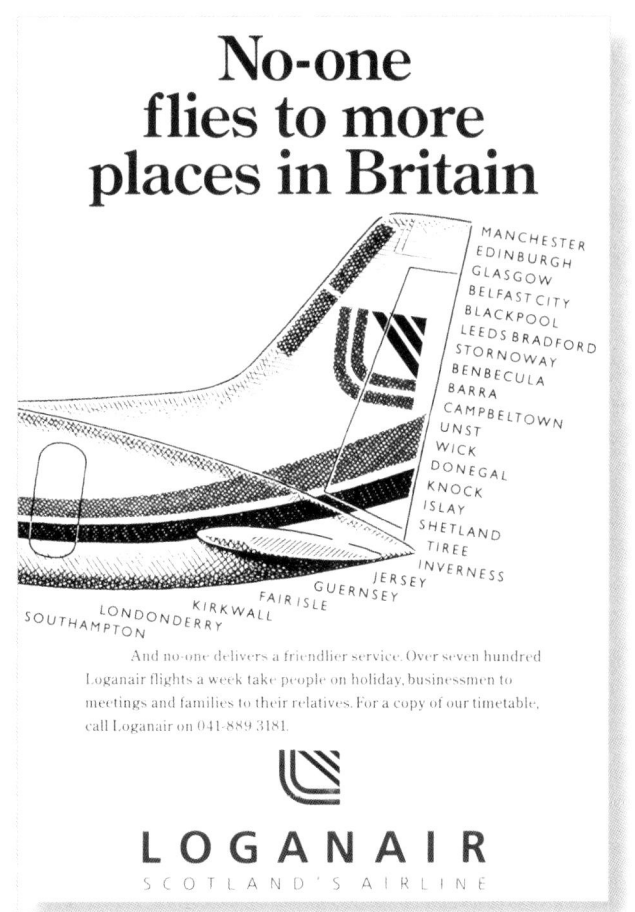

Issued by:	Place of Issue	ABERDEEN		Place of Issue	
BRITISH WORLD AIRLINES				Flight coupon **2** Return journey	
VISCOUNT HOUSE SOUTHEND AIRPORT, ESSEX SS2 6YL	Issued subject to conditions of contract overleaf Not refundable	Ticket no.	:129:069	Ticket no.	:129:069
Passenger ticket and baggage check		Issue Date	10 AUG 95	Passenger name WOODLEY/C MR	

From ABERDEEN	Carrier	Flight	Departure Date	Departure Time	CH'KD PCS.	Weight Kgs.	UnCh'kd Kgs	Flight no. BWL 85
To EDINBURGH	BWL	8503	10AUG95	0955				Date 10 AUG 95 Time OPEN
To ABERDEEN	BWL	OPEN		—				From EDINBURGH To ABERDEEN

Baggage allowance kgs. (nil for infants)	Passenger name WOODLEY / C MR	NOT TRANSFERABLE	Baggage	kgs.	Pcs.

NOTICE If the passenger's journey involves an ultimate destination or stop in a country other than the country of departure the Warsaw Convention may be applicable and the Convention governs and in most cases limits the liability of carriers for death or personal injury and in respect of loss of or damage to baggage.

M	F	C	I

FROM GLASGOW	DAYS	DEP	ARR	FLT NO	AIRCRAFT	VIA
TO BFS	12345	0730	0315	792	D0228	Non Stop
TO BFS	12345	1335	1420	796	D0228	Non Stop
TO BFS	12345	1630	1715	794	D0228	Non Stop
TO BFS	12345	1835	1920	777	D0228	Non Stop

FROM BELFAST	DAYS	DEP	ARR	FLT NO	AIRCRAFT	VIA
TO GLA	23456	0245	0325	791	D0228	Non Stop
TO GLA	12345	0830	0910	716	D0228	Non Stop
TO GLA	12345	1435	1515	799	D0228	Non Stop
TO GLA	12345	1730	1810	795	D0228	Non Stop

FROM GLASGOW	DAYS	DEP	ARR	FLT NO	AIRCRAFT	VIA
TO ABZ	12345	0925	1010	716	D0228	Non Stop
TO ABZ	12345	1625	1710	799	D0228	Non Stop

FROM ABERDEEN	DAYS	DEP	ARR	FLT NO	AIRCRAFT	VIA
TO GLA	12345	1230	1320	796	D0228	Non Stop
TO GLA	12345	1730	1820	777	D0228	Non Stop

FROM ABERDEEN	DAYS	DEP	ARR	FLT NO	AIRCRAFT	VIA
TO BFS	12345	1230	1420	796	D0228	Glasgow
TO BFS	12345	1730	1920	777	D0228	Glasgow

FROM BELFAST	DAYS	DEP	ARR	FLT NO	AIRCRAFT	VIA
TO ABZ	12345	0830	1015	716	D0228	Glasgow
TO ABZ	12345	1435*	1715	799	D0228	Glasgow

*1.15 Stopover Glasgow

USEFUL TELEPHONE NUMBERS

MALINAIR	Reservations	041 887 1181
	Head Office	041 887 1151

AIRPORTS

Aberdeen	0224 722331
Belfast International	0232 229271
Carrickfinn	010353 7548284
Gatwick	0293 28822
Glasgow	041 887 1111
Teeside	0325 332811

HANDLING AGENTS

at Belfast — Servisair	08494 22701
at Gatwick — Caledonian Aviation Services	0293 31144
at Glasgow — Servisair	041 887 1381
at Teeside — Servisair	0325 332514
at Humberside — Spurnair	0652 680430
at Manchester — Servisair	061 489 3251

Malinair timetable.

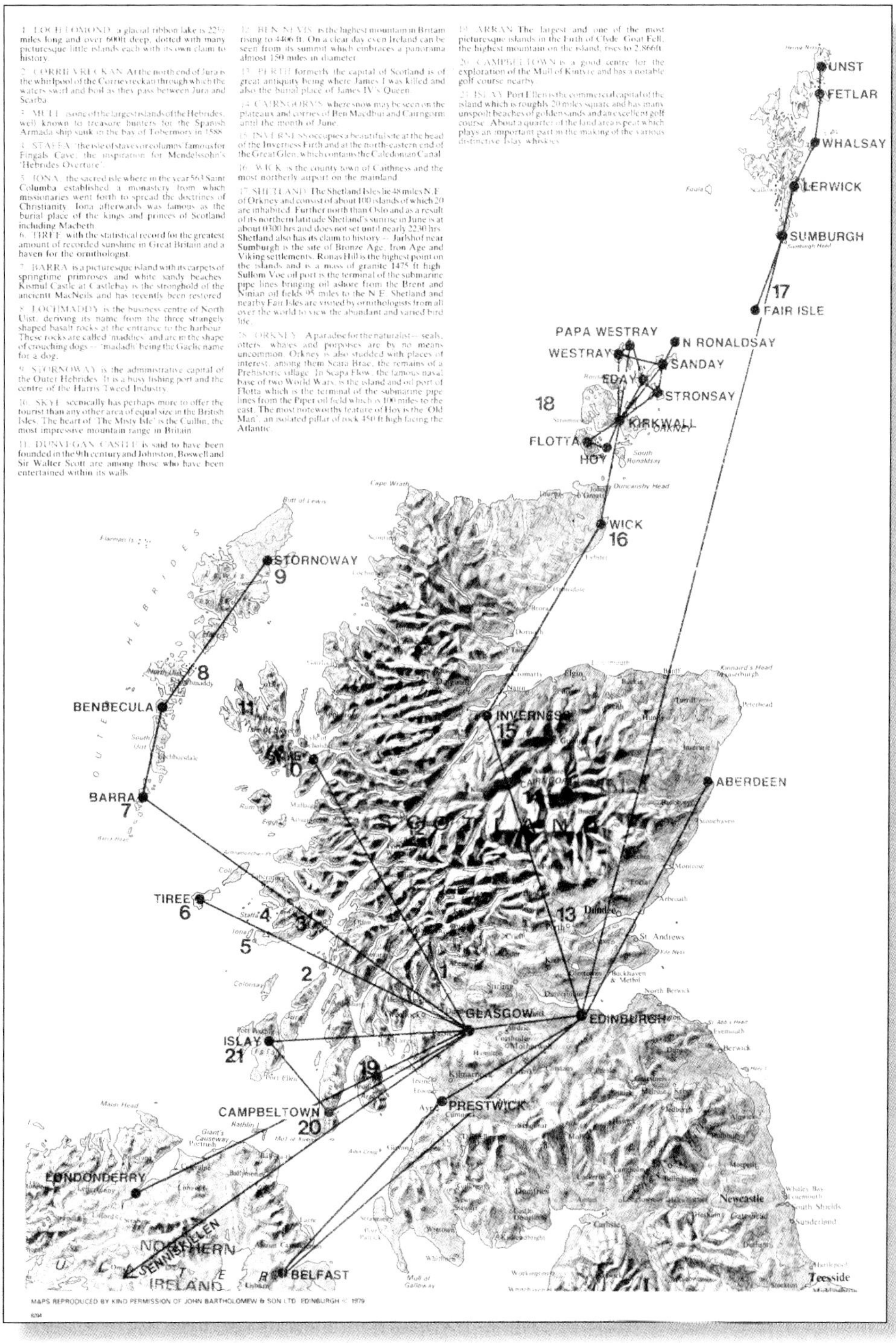

1. LOCH LOMOND a glacial ribbon lake is 22½ miles long and over 600ft deep, dotted with many picturesque little islands each with its own claim to history.

2. CORRIEVRECKAN At the north end of Jura is the whirlpool of the Corrievreckan through which the waters swirl and boil as they pass between Jura and Scarba.

3. MULL is one of the largest islands of the Hebrides, well known to treasure hunters for the Spanish Armada ship sunk in the bay of Tobermory in 1588.

4. STAFFA the isle of staves or columns famous for Fingal's Cave, the inspiration for Mendelssohn's 'Hebrides Overture'.

5. IONA the sacred isle where in the year 563 Saint Columba established a monastery from which missionaries went forth to spread the doctrines of Christianity. Iona afterwards was famous as the burial place of the kings and princes of Scotland including Macbeth.

6. TIREE with the statistical record for the greatest amount of recorded sunshine in Great Britain and a haven for the ornithologist.

7. BARRA is a picturesque island with its carpets of springtime primroses and white sandy beaches. Kismul Castle at Castlebay is the stronghold of the ancient MacNeils and has recently been restored.

8. LOCHMADDY is the business centre of North Uist, deriving its name from the three strangely shaped basalt rocks at the entrance to the harbour. These rocks are called 'maddies' and are in the shape of crouching dogs — madadh being the Gaelic name for a dog.

9. STORNOWAY is the administrative capital of the Outer Hebrides. It is a busy fishing port and the centre of the Harris Tweed Industry.

10. SKYE scenically has perhaps more to offer the tourist than any other area of equal size in the British Isles. The heart of 'The Misty Isle' is the Cuillin, the most impressive mountain range in Britain.

11. DUNVEGAN CASTLE is said to have been founded in the 9th century and Johnston, Boswell and Sir Walter Scott are among those who have been entertained within its walls.

12. BEN NEVIS is the highest mountain in Britain rising to 4406 ft. On a clear day even Ireland can be seen from its summit which embraces a panorama almost 150 miles in diameter.

13. PERTH formerly the capital of Scotland is of great antiquity being where James I was killed and also the burial place of James IV's Queen.

14. CAIRNGORMS where snow may be seen on the plateaux and corries of Ben Macdhui and Cairngorm until the month of June.

15. INVERNESS occupies a beautiful site at the head of the Inverness Firth and at the north-eastern end of the Great Glen, which contains the Caledonian Canal.

16. WICK is the county town of Caithness and the most northerly airport on the mainland.

17. SHETLAND The Shetland Isles lie 48 miles N.E. of Orkney and consist of about 100 islands of which 20 are inhabited. Further north than Oslo and as a result of its northern latitude Shetland's sunrise in June is at about 0300 hrs and does not set until nearly 2230 hrs. Shetland also has its claim to history — Jarlshof near Sumburgh is the site of Bronze Age, Iron Age and Viking settlements. Ronas Hill is the highest point on the islands and is a mass of granite 1475 ft high. Sullom Voe oil port is the terminal of the submarine pipe lines bringing oil ashore from the Brent and Ninian oil fields 95 miles to the N.E. Shetland and nearby Fair Isle are visited by ornithologists from all over the world to view the abundant and varied bird life.

18. ORKNEY A paradise for the naturalist — seals, otters, whales and porpoises are by no means uncommon. Orkney is also studded with places of interest, among them Skara Brae, the remains of a Prehistoric village. In Scapa Flow, the famous naval base of two World Wars, is the island and oil port of Flotta which is the terminal of the submarine pipe lines from the Piper oil field which is 100 miles to the east. The most noteworthy feature of Hoy is the 'Old Man', an isolated pillar of rock 450 ft high facing the Atlantic.

19. ARRAN The largest and one of the most picturesque islands in the Firth of Clyde. Goat Fell, the highest mountain on the island, rises to 2866ft.

20. CAMPBELTOWN is a good centre for the exploration of the Mull of Kintyre and has a notable golf course nearby.

21. ISLAY Port Ellen is the commercial capital of the island which is roughly 20 miles square and has many unspoilt beaches of golden sands and an excellent golf course. About a quarter of the land area is peat which plays an important part in the making of the various distinctive Islay whiskies.

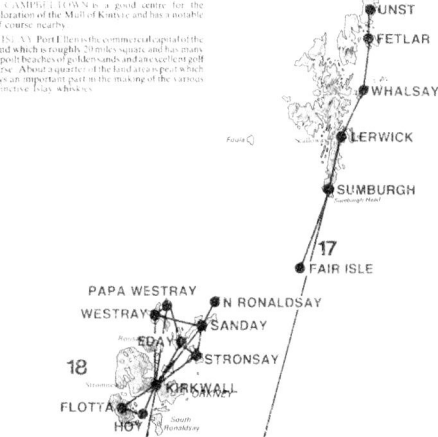

UNST
FETLAR
WHALSAY
LERWICK
SUMBURGH
17 FAIR ISLE
PAPA WESTRAY   N RONALDSAY
WESTRAY   SANDAY
EDAY   STRONSAY
18   KIRKWALL
FLOTTA
HOY
WICK 16
STORNOWAY 9
8
BENBECULA   11
10
BARRA 7
TIREE 6   4   3
5
2
ISLAY 21
19
CAMPBELTOWN 20
PRESTWICK
INVERNESS 15
ABERDEEN
13 Dundee
GLASGOW   EDINBURGH
LONDONDERRY
NORTHERN IRELAND
BELFAST

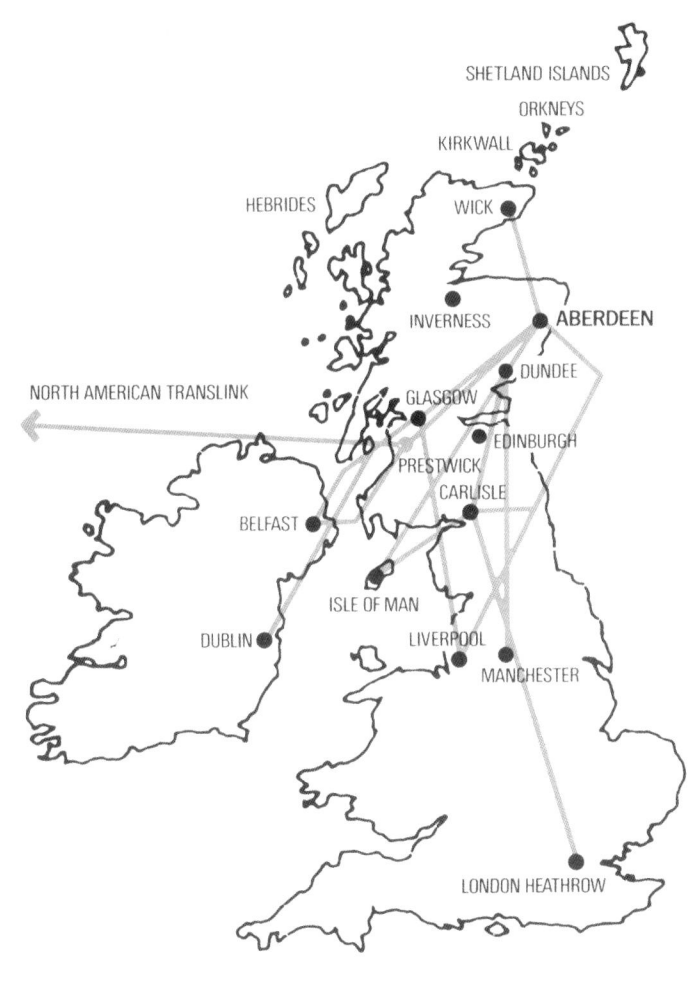

A WEE NIP HERALDS MAJOR CONTRACTS FROM AMERADA HESS, DIAMOND DRILLING AND MARATHON OIL

NEWSLETTER

WINTER 94/95

It seems as though it was just yesterday when Bon Accord Airways took delivery of Shorts 360 aircraft G-CLAS fresh from major overhaul by Caledonian Airborne Engineering at Aberdeen but it is now well over twelve months since the aircraft was placed in service and many interesting contract and charter operations have been undertaken since then.

Bon Accord was granted a Class A licence by the Civil Aviation Authority in mid-July 1993 and our first flight with the 360 was a company outing from Edinburgh to Islay to visit a distillery ' Contract flying was undertaken for Diamond Drilling between Aberdeen and Brest, France and for Ross Offshore between Aberdeen, Newcastle and Esbjerg. A major contract was awarded by Amerada Hess in September 1993 for 100 flights between Aberdeen and Sumburgh and Bon Accord is delighted that the next phase of exploration by Amerada Hess results in continued use of our versatile 360 aircraft to and from Sumburgh and Aberdeen from September 1994.

In between the regular contract flights G-CLAS has operated a remarkable variety of ad hoc charters including a day trip to Leeds for Grampian Regional Council, rugby supporters to Dublin for the weekend, a party of doctors to Guernsey for a weekend convention, several subcharters for

British Airways, Air UK, Manx Airlines and Business Air. German tourists from Wick to Manchester following a fabulous weekend at Ackergill Tower near Wick, a party of South Americans from Paris to Edinburgh (their inbound flight was twelve hours late and they had missed their connecting service), a party of Japanese golfers on a UK tour from Aberdeen to Shannon who amused guests at their

Aberdeen hotel with a display of fisticuffs and the owners and families of a Shetland fishing company between Sumburgh and Molde, Norway, for the launch of a brand new trawler. Bon Accord also came to the rescue of over 100 stranded tourists unable to travel from Southampton to Jersey as their hydrofoil was stormbound and we flew them safely to their holiday destination.

MORE POWER WHEN IT'S NEEDED

From March 1994 Bon Accord operated a short term contract on behalf of Stena A/S of Norway flying oil rig personnel between Aberdeen, Edinburgh and Stavanger and this was followed in July by a contract from Marathon Oil UK Ltd for crew change flights to and from Swansea and Aberdeen in support of exploration by the oil rig Sedco 711. The South Wales airport is due considerable praise for the support services provided for our 360 aircraft and the KLM helicopter which operated the offshore flights.

Our Shorts 360 aircraft is proving to be ideal for crew change operations and we are particularly pleased that our aircraft is fitted with PT65 AR engines as compared to the standard 65R engines more common with other 360 operators. The 65AR engines provide more power when it is necessary

and this is most beneficial for operations to and from the likes of Sumburgh where the runways are short, or when aircraft systems, such as de icing, place additional demands on the engines. The 360 is a very cost effective aeroplane and has the lowest costs in comparison to aircraft of similar capacity. With a still air flight time between Aberdeen and Sumburgh, for example of only 59 minutes, pressurised aircraft in the present financial climate, are an expensive luxury. Bon Accord Airways is celebrating its second anniversary and is now very firmly established as an airline with the ability to react quickly and efficiently to a variety of charter requirements be it standing on the ramp of a Scottish airport for filming purposes or a long term contract flying oil rig personnel for the major companies of the oil industry.

tel: (01224) 772234 or 722331   fax: (01224) 772523

SPREADING OUR WINGS and FLYING HIGH.

Scheduled Services

The addition of two BAe 748 pressurised turboprop airliners to our fleet of Gulfstream 1 aircraft enables us to offer even more capacity on our scheduled flights between Aberdeen, Edinburgh and East Midlands, with our popular 24 seat Gulfstream turboprop operating to and from Aberdeen and Manchester.

Our Scheduled Services are timed to offer the businessman the maximum possible business day whether it be in Aberdeen, Edinburgh, East Midlands or Manchester and our departures are timed so that it is not necessary to rise at unearthly hours of the morning.

With a variety of aircraft at our disposal we can meet the special needs of clients who wish to undertake private charter at times convenient to themselves and to locations outwith our scheduled routes.

Our fleet of passenger aircraft offer a capacity from 10 to 44 seats and, in addition, we provide aircraft for the carriage of cargo or mail.

We are available for ad hoc charter, long or short term contract flying, wet or dry lease.

Our vast experience in the care, maintenance and operation of a wide variety of aircraft makes us the obvious choice for those who wish to retain their own private aircraft.

Let Aberdeen Airways provide the support services which are necessary. Air crews, cabin staff, maintenance engineers are available to the private user so that your own aircraft may be always ready for your immediate use when and where it is required.

"Profitable growth needs the support of an experienced and multi-disciplined team. Our new set-up gives us that tremendous additional drive for long-term expansion."

Jim Bicker
managing director,
Aberdeen Airways.

Aircraft Management

Aberdeen Airways operate the only CAA approved fixed-wing maintenance facility in Aberdeen. Our large modern hangar provides 27,000 square feet of covered accommodation and outside 40,000 square feet of parking space. Our experienced team of fully qualified engineers can handle all major maintenance programmes on turboprop and piston engined aircraft. Our paint division offers a complete aircraft refurbishing service and can produce an external finish on helicopters and aircraft which is to the highest standard. We also provide Avgas aviation fuel for piston engined aircraft.

Reservations

Our reservations unit is fully computerised and part of the Travicom/Galileo system with our staff currently accepting in excess of 40,000 individual reservations every year. We are still able however to offer a reservations service to smaller airlines who may not wish to invest in computer facilities until their own services are well established. As part of our reservations facility we also provide a full revenue accounting service.

Engineering

BIBLIOGRAPHY

In the preparation for this book I have plundered many books and websites, including the following:

Iain Hutchison, *The Story of Loganair*. Western Isles Publishing Co., 1987.

The Shetland News. Issue of 25 July 2006.

Peter V. Clegg, *Flying Against The Elements*. 1987.

Phil Lo Bao, *An Illustrated History of British European Airways*. Browcom Group, 1989.

Phil Lo Bao and Iain Hutchison, *BEAline to the Islands*. Kea Publishing, 2002.

James D. Ferguson, *The Story of Aberdeen Airport*. Scottish Airports, 1984.

Peter V Clegg, *Sword In The Sky*. 1990.

The Orcadian Online Archive.

Alan Whitfield, *Island Pilot*. The Shetland Times, 1995.

A.C. Merton Jones, *British Independent Airlines Since 1946*, first edition. LAAS International/ Merseyside Aviation Society, 1976.

Bradshaw's *International Air Guide*, 15 February–14 March 1952.

Keith McCloskey, *Edinburgh Airport: A History*. Tempus Publishing, 2006.

Peter Berry MRaeS, *Prestwick Airport and Scottish Aviation*. Tempus Publishing, 2005.

Guy Halford MacLeod, *Britain's Airlines Volume One 1946–1951*. Tempus Publishing, 2006.

The airliners.net website.

The Aviation Safety Network website.